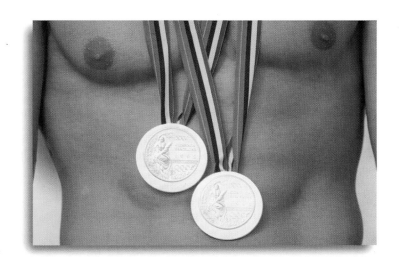

100
Greatest Moments
In Olympic History

100
Greatest Moments

General Publishing Group, Inc.

Los Angeles

In Olympic History

By Bud Greenspan

Publisher, W. Quay Hays
Managing Editor, Colby Allerton
Art Director, Kurt Wahlner
Production Director, Nadeen Torio
Color & Pre-Press Director, Gaston Moraga
Copy Editor, Diane Woo

100 Greatest Moments in Olympic History
is published by
General Publishing Group, Inc.,
2701 Ocean Park Blvd., Ste. 140, CA 90405
310-314-4000

Library of Congress Cataloging-in-Publication Data

Greenspan, Bud.
    100 greatest moments in Olympic history / by Bud Greenspan.
    Special Centennial Edition
        p. cm
    ISBN 1-881649-66-0 (alk. paper)
    1. Olympics--History I. Title.
    GV721.5.G65 1995
    796.48--dc20   95-35062
                                                    CIP
                                                    AC

10 9 8 7 6 5 4 3 2 1

Printed in Italy

Very special thanks to:

Val Ching and Tony Duffy at Allsport, and the Allsport London offices; Pat Olkiewicz and Barry King at the United States Olympic Committee; Wayne Wilson, Karen Goddy and the staff at the Amateur Athletic Foundation of Los Angeles; Bill Bennett and John Dolak at UCLA; Terry Kent at the U.S. Bobsled and Skeleton Federation; Nancy Moore at USA Shooting; Vanessa Osborne, Michael Lira, Brad Slepack, Lindsay Murai and all persons involved in the completion of this project.

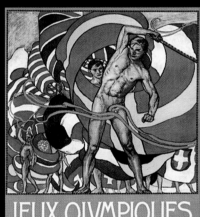

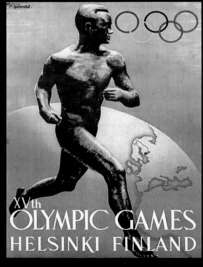

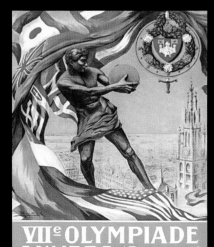

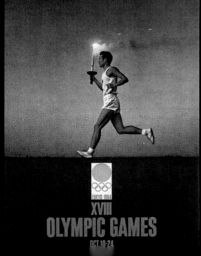

Contents

Introduction

by Juan Antonio Samaranch
President of the International Olympic Committee

It is indeed a pleasure for the IOC President to write the introduction to Bud Greenspan's *100 Greatest Moments in Olympic History*, moments which are cherished by the people of the world.

Mr. Bud Greenspan has chronicled the history of the Olympic Movement for more than four decades, keeping alive the flame of Olympism for thousands of athletes and millions of spectators today and for generations to come.

He has created intimate portrayals of young men and women as athletes, and more importantly as human beings who strive to overcome personal challenges, bringing honor to themselves, their country and most importantly, honor to us all.

Mr. Greenspan has been called the foremost producer, writer and director of Olympic films; more than that, he is an everlasting friend of the Olympic family.

It was in the City of Rome in 1985, after the premiere showing of his film *16 Days of Glory—Los Angeles,* his five-hour Official Film of the 1984 Olympic Games, that I presented to Bud Greenspan the Olympic Order for his outstanding achievements and service to the Olympic Movement.

It is right and proper then, on the eve of the Centennial Games celebration of the modern era, the Games of the XXVI Olympiad in Atlanta, to pay tribute to the man who has captured the heart and the humanity of the Olympics in words and on film and who has now compiled some of these most stirring portraits in this written work, *100 Greatest Moments in Olympic History.*

On behalf of the Olympic Movement, I would like to express our most heartfelt gratitude to Bud Greenspan for writing his *100 Greatest Moments in Olympic History* and his lifelong commitment to the perpetuation of the Olympic spirit.

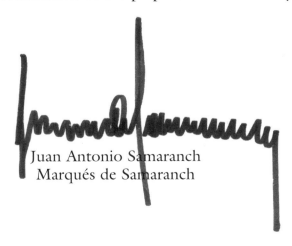

Juan Antonio Samaranch
Marqués de Samaranch

Foreword

by William Porter Payne

President and CEO, The Atlanta Committee for the Olympic Games

Bud Greenspan's vision is unlike that of anyone else on this earth. His eyes function not through his brain but through his heart.

When most of us look at an Olympic athlete, we see a highly tuned physique. Bud's eyes see a human being. We are impressed by finely sculpted muscles; he reveres the discipline and endurance that created those muscles. While we witness the athlete's skills, Bud is taking note of the pride and persistence that developed those skills. And when we watch intense athletic competition, Bud experiences the pure joy of the contest.

It is his uncanny knack for capturing the human drama of sports that has created our vista of shared memories from the Olympic Games. In fact, Bud Greenspan's work and the Olympic Games are synonymous. Now we all can enjoy his vision through his latest work, *100 Greatest Moments in Olympic History.*

Many people have attended every Olympic Summer Games since 1948, as has Bud, but it is Bud's vision that has contributed to our most heartfelt memories. He has spoiled us by intimately sharing what would be otherwise untold, gripping and emotional stories of triumph and tragedy. We learn about Denmark's Lis Hartel, who battles her way out of paralysis in 1952 to be the first woman to win a silver medal in equestrian dressage. And we will never forget John Stephen Akhwari, a marathon runner from Tanzania. His bloody and bandaged form hobbled through the last stretches of the marathon in Mexico City because, he says, his country sent him to finish the race, not just start it.

These stories teach us great lessons in human courage and perseverance. Bud's common thread is the showcasing of the human spirit. Perhaps this is the element that makes his work appealing to everyone, not just those of us who love sports.

Bud Greenspan consistently communicates the humanity of the Olympic Games around the world. His great talent is uncovering those little known stories of individual heroics. How he does this remains a mystery, yet it is a mystery best left unsolved. As his dramas unfold, he touches the highest aspirations of us all through his philosophy that some champions finish last and that winners are not the only heroes. This philosophy goes to the very heart of the Olympic belief that to compete is the highest form of victory.

In the years leading up to the creation of The Atlanta Committee for the Olympic Games and our efforts to host the Centennial Olympic Games, I have watched Bud's films many times. During each viewing, I experience a new emotion, and I see the Olympic Games in a way that is slightly different from before. In fact, Bud's portrayal of the human spirit fueled my desire to be a part of this great endeavor. It is as if Bud Greenspan captured my dreams on film.

Our anticipation of the Centennial Olympic Games grows as we come closer to the moment the Torch is illuminated at Olympic Stadium in Atlanta. These Games will be the greatest experience of my life, and I know my Olympic memories will be enhanced because of Bud's genius.

In the meantime, Bud shares with us through this book his unique vision of historic Olympic Games. You hold in your hands the essence of all that is good and pure about Olympic Games competition. Through Bud's eyes, you will feel the pride and the persistence, grasp the discipline and endurance and, most importantly, experience the joy.

Billy Payne

President and CEO
The Atlanta Committee for the Olympic Games

Prologue

Selecting any list of greatest moments is at best subjective — particularly those that occurred in sporting events. "Greatest" becomes increasingly difficult when an event such as the Olympic Games is a century old and filled with extraordinary achievements.

Therefore, the word "greatest" could be transposed easily with the word "memorable" — those dramatic, humanistic, inspiring happenings that affected me personally in my life's work — to chronicle the men, women and events who personify the Olympic philosophy — "there are no great people, rather there are great challenges that ordinary people are forced to meet."

In the summer of 1964 Jesse Owens and his wife, Ruth, and my wife, Cappy, and I arrived in West Berlin to film our one hour documentary *Jesse Owens Returns to Berlin*. The idea for making a film on Jesse's life actually began thirteen years earlier in the summer of 1951 after reading an article in the *New York Times*.

The article, datelined Berlin, Germany told of the exploits of the Harlem Globetrotter basketball team, which was performing one of its exhibitions before 80,000 people at the Berlin Olympic Stadium — the scene of the 1936 Olympic Games.

At halftime, as thousands of the spectators left their seats for refreshments, the loudspeaker announcer stopped everyone in their tracks.

"Ladies and gentlemen," the public address system blared throughout the stadium. "Please return to your seats. Now entering through the marathon gate I give you the champion of champions . . . Jesse Owens!"

Onto the field came 36-year-old Jesse Owens, wearing the same uniform he had worn during his four great gold medal performances fifteen years earlier. Now these many years later he was given the opportunity to take a "victory lap" — the ceremonial run around the track he was not permitted to take in 1936 when the Nazi hierarchy, Hitler, Goering, Goebbels and Hess, looked down upon the field.

Incredibly, the red cinder track was untouched by Allied bombing during World War II. As Jesse smilingly and effortlessly moved around the track a chant began . . . "JESSE OWENS . . . JESSE OWENS . . . JESSE OWENS . . . ." It started as a small rumble and then reverberated through every section of the stadium. The louder the chant became, the more Jesse waved to the crowd.

Soon Jesse completed his run around the 400 meter track and slowly trotted toward a first row box situated beneath the veranda that fifteen years earlier was the vantage point of Adolf Hitler. This time he was greeted by Ernst Reuter, the mayor of West Berlin. Reuter held up his hand and the crowd quieted. He then picked up the microphone.

"Jesse Owens . . . fifteen years ago Hitler refused to shake your hand," he said. "I will try to make up for it today by taking both of them."

Mayor Reuter reached out and embraced Jesse and the crowd responded with a mighty roar. Jesse then trotted out of the arena as the crowd continued to cry out, "JESSE OWENS . . . JESSE OWENS . . . JESSE OWENS . . . ."

I was chilled after reading the article and knew that someday I would make use of it. So it was in the summer of 1964, thirteen years later, that I found myself with my camera crew in the mammoth empty Berlin Olympic Stadium to start the filming of *Jesse Owens Returns to Berlin*, a one hour television documentary.

It was an eerie feeling standing in the empty stadium where Jesse's victories had upset the Nazi propaganda theory of the master race. Standing there you could all but hear the cries of "Seig Heil" as the audience paid homage to Adolf Hitler. Then, too, one could imagine 80,000 voices singing "Deutschland Uber Alles" that was part of the climax of the opening day ceremonies and played every time a German winner stood on the top step of the victory platform during the Games.

On the second day of filming, I took Jesse over to the starting line of the 100 meters — the scene of his four victories.

I wanted Jesse to be as relaxed and informal as possible, so I didn't prepare him in advance for the questions I would ask.

"Jesse," I said, "what was it like as you were one of six finalists in the 100 meters as the

German starter shouted out the command, 'Auf die platze, on your mark . . . Fertig, set . . .' just before the sound of the starting gun?"

Without hesitation Jesse replied, "Bud, it was a lifetime of training for just 10 seconds . . . ."

His simple answer became the philosophy of the film and all the future Olympic films I would produce — to pay honor to all those thousands of young men and women who enter the arena, make the attempt and pursue excellence. And because of them, all of us go back to our homes the better for it.

His words would forever remind me that we must pay attention to all those marvelous athletes who give so much of their lives so that we can enjoy the celebration that history will recall as "16 Days of Glory." The Olympic Games is not just the story of those who make it to the victory podium, but those many thousands who fail to gain Olympic immortality by an infinitesimal part of an inch or a fraction of a second.

I have been to every Olympic Games since the 1948 London Games as a broadcaster, journalist and film maker. In addition I have gathered rare film dating back to the 1908 London Games, and our library consists of more than two million feet of film.

Through the decades in producing more than 100 Olympic films, I've traveled throughout the world interviewing the great and near great who competed in the earliest of the modern Olympics.

When America's 1,500 meter silver medal winner at the 1912 Stockholm Games, Abel Kiviat, had passed his 91st birthday, we took him back to the scene of his performance. There, more than seven decades later, he was able to recount vividly the Olympic experience of an era long since gone.

We are able to relive the 1936 Berlin Olympics through the eyes of the immortal Jesse Owens, who returned to Berlin with us to recount his four magnificent victories in what history has termed "the Nazi Olympics." And we are able to cheer again the dramatic victory of America's Billy Mills in the Tokyo 1964 10,000 run — one of the great upset wins of modern Olympic history. And we are able to recount the agonizing journey of John Stephen Akhwari of Tanzania — the last man to finish the marathon at the 1968 Mexico City Games, who had the courage and dedication, though severely injured, to finish the race with glory.

So this book is dedicated to the many who through the past century have entered the arena and competed with honor — those who dare valiantly to reach for the heavens — not those alone who were fortunate to grab hold of their star. For it has been written, "The Honor should not alone go to those who have not fallen; rather all Honor to those who fall and rise again."

Acknowledgements

To Sydney Thayer, whose dedicated research made life easier — assisted by Buena Guzman and Baptiste Caraux.

Dan Rarback and Ann Russell for their tireless effort in making our deadline.

Tony Duffy and ALL SPORT for searching their archives for the dramatic photographs.

A special thanks to Wayne Wilson of the Amateur Athletic Foundation, who always had the time for us in researching rare photographs.

To my editor, Colby Allerton, whose suggestions were always "right on."

To art director Kurt Wahlner, for making the book a visual success.

To my friend, George Wallach, who brought us all together.

To Bill Mallon and Erich Kamper, authors of *The Golden Book of the Olympic Games*, for their courtesy in permitting us to reproduce sections from their definitive collection of all-time Olympic records.

And finally, to my old friend Jeffrey Cokin, who keeps us off welfare.

Dedication

To Nancy Beffa—

My partner in life who makes so many lovely things happen—who showed me that the "impossible" just takes a little longer.

The most important thing
in the Olympic Games
is not to win but to
take part, just as the most
important thing in life
is not the triumph
but the struggle.
The essential thing is not
to have conquered
but to have fought well.

–The Olympic Creed

Let the Games Begin. . .

18

Jesse Owens
Berlin, 1936

One year before the 1936 Berlin Olympics, Jesse Owens had thrilled the world by setting three world records and equaling a fourth in a single afternoon track meet in Ann Arbor, Michigan. His Olympic triumphs in the 100 meters, long jump and 200 meters and as leadoff man in the 4 x 100 relay in Berlin have been well documented, but very few accounts captured how close Jesse was to leaving the Olympics with only two gold medals.

"The German champion Luz Long saved me in the long jump," said Jesse. "In the qualifying round we had three attempts to make it to the final, but I fouled twice. I was scared stiff that I would blow it on my third and last attempt to qualify and not make it to the final. Then Long came over to me and in broken English said, 'Jesse, let me make a suggestion. I will place my towel a foot in front of the foul line and you can use this for your takeoff. You should then qualify easily.'"

Jesse took Long's advice, and since the qualifying distance was three feet less than the distance Jesse normally leaped, he qualified easily and then went on to defeat the German champion in the field.

"It was so gracious of him," Jesse recalled solemnly. "After my victory was secure, Luz was the first one to greet me, and we walked arm in arm right in front of Hitler's box. Hitler must have gone crazy watching us embrace. The sad part of the story is I never saw Luz Long again. He was killed in World War II."

Jesse wasn't supposed to be a member of the relay team. But in a controversy that still goes on today, he was ordered to run when two Jewish teammates, Marty Glickman and Sam Stoller, were removed from the team under cloudy circumstances. "We had a team meeting a day before the relay final and were told by our coaches that Glickman and Stoller would not run," remembered Jesse. "We were stunned. The rumor was that the Nazi hierarchy asked our officials not to humiliate them further by using two Jewish athletes to add to the gold medals black athletes had already won. I protested, saying, 'I've won three gold medals, let Marty and Sam have their chance.' Quickly and forcefully I was told to shut up. We won the relay by ten meters, but we would have won just as easily with Marty and Sam."

It appeared that hundreds of young German frauleins weren't aware that 22-year-old Jesse Owens was happily married and the father of a small daughter when he won his four gold medals at those Olympics. Even if they knew, they didn't care. He laughingly recalled receiving dozens of perfumed letters daily offering secret love trysts from enamored German girls who couldn't care less about Adolf Hitler's Aryan racial philosophy of a master race.

Jesse's record of four track and field gold medals in the same Olympics held for 48 years until Carl Lewis duplicated that feat at the 1984 Los Angeles Olympics in the same four events.

With the help of his German opponent, Luz Long (right), Jesse Owens went on to win the gold in the long jump.

Mary Lou Retton

On the evening of August 3, 1984, 36 finalists for the individual all-around women's gymnastic title were introduced to the 13,000 spectators that jammed Pauley Pavilion at the Los Angeles Olympics. Four events would be contested: uneven bars, balance beam, vault and floor exercise.

The gymnasts were divided into four groups of nine so that each apparatus could be contested simultaneously. The favorite to win the gold was Ecaterina Szabó of Romania. Sixteen-year-old Mary Lou Retton was considered America's best hope for a medal. Four foot nine inches tall and weighing 92 pounds, Retton had never taken part in a major international competition before the Los Angeles Games.

Ironically, Retton's coach was Bela Karolyi, who defected from Romania a few years earlier. Karolyi's most famous pupil was Nadia Comaneci, who at the 1976 Montreal Games received seven perfect "tens" on her way to winning three gold medals, including the all-around championship. Comaneci's "tens" were the first ever awarded in Olympic gymnastics.

Retton's road to the Olympics was a difficult one. She missed the 1983 World Championships because of a bad wrist, and six weeks before the Los Angeles Games she had arthroscopic surgery to remove bone chips.

Retton was in first place, fifteen hundredths of a point in front of Szabó even before the individual all-around competition began.

By gymnastic rules half of each gymnast's individual total gained earlier in the team competition, which was won by Romania with the United States second, is carried over in the battle for the individual all-around. Retton slightly outscored Szabó in the team championship.

In the individual all-around, Retton and Szabó were in different groups and therefore competing on different apparatus at the same time.

On the first apparatus Szabó scored a perfect ten on the balance beam. Retton performed well on the uneven bars but not good enough to remain alone in first place. After the first round they were tied for the lead.

Szabó performed an almost flawless floor exercise — scoring a 9.95 to Retton's 9.80 on the balance beam. Szabó now led by fifteen hundredths of a point.

On her third apparatus, the vault, Szabó was awarded 9.90 but the crowd roared its approval as the judges gave Retton a perfect ten in the floor exercise. With one apparatus left, Retton still trailed the Romanian by five hundredths of a point.

Szabó was given a 9.90 on the uneven bars, finishing just before Retton was to step up for the vault, her last apparatus.

The situation was now clear. If Retton scored a perfect ten on the vault, the gold medal was hers. A 9.95 would tie Retton with the Romanian and they would share the gold medal. Anything less, and the gold medal would go to Szabó.

"You're going to do it. . . you're going to do it!" chanted Karolyi to his pupil as Retton received last minute instructions from her coach. "I know you can do it. The best you can vault. I know you can do it. . . Now or never. OK?" Much calmer than her coach, Mary Lou responded with a smiling, "OK," and moved to the mat.

The crowd was deadly silent as Mary Lou eyed the apparatus, then began her run. She hit the "horse" strongly, with both hands, twirled through the air, then "stuck" her landing. The crowd roared hysterically but Karolyi's screaming could be heard above the incredible noise.

"Ten, ten, ten . . . ten!" he screamed over and over.

Thirty seconds went by before the score was flashed throughout the stadium. Karolyi was correct, Mary Lou Retton had scored a perfect "ten" and was Olympic champion — the first American gymnast to ever win the overall title.

There was one final dramatic moment that became lost through the passage of time. By gymnastic rules, each contestant is given two attempts at the vault, and the highest mark is the one recognized. With her victory in hand, Mary Lou did not have to make a second attempt. But she did anyway. She again received a perfect "ten."

Torvill & Dean

Perhaps if they had not met, Jayne Torvill might today be working in an insurance office and Christopher Dean might still be walking the streets of Nottingham City as a police constable, an unlikely background for Great Britain's legendary ice dancing pair — still considered the greatest team in the history of the sport.

When they finished fifth at the 1980 Lake Placid Games, there was nothing to indicate that their future greatness would all but eliminate their first names. In the years that followed, the press and public would refer to them simply as Torvill and Dean.

After the Lake Placid Games Torvill and Dean won three world championships, all highlighted by ultimate performances of grace, fluency and particularly invention.

"We don't want to do anything plain if we can put in something interesting," said Christopher Dean. "If something looks plain, it is wrong."

At the Helsinki 1983 world championships the duo performed brilliantly, though both were painfully injured. Twice in practice sessions Jayne fell badly and had to have her back and shoulder strapped. Dean too was physically impaired, having to undergo treatment twice a day for fluid in his knee.

Their victory under such adverse conditions at the world championships set the stage for their becoming the overwhelming favorites for the upcoming 1984 Sarajevo Olympics.

Ice dancing is divided into three separate sessions — two compulsory dances that account for 20% of the final score, original set pattern dance worth 30% and finally "free dance," or as the pair skaters call it, "the let yourself go" program, worth 50%.

Torvill and Dean were comfortably in front after the first two sections of competition. If they played it "safe" the victory was theirs. But complacency was not in the Torvill and Dean vocabulary — rather, their inspiration was the age-old Olympic motto, "Citius, Altius, Fortius." Swifter, Higher, Stronger . . . .

Skating to Ravel's *Bolero*, Torvill and Dean brought pairs ice dancing to a height beyond the realm of imagination. When the scores were flashed for artistic impression, all nine judges awarded them a perfect six — a mark that most believe will never be reached again — and with it the 1984 Olympic ice dancing gold medal.

24

Dorando Pietri London, 1908 Italy

The marathon race at the 1908 London Olympics is historic for two reasons. First, it was there that the official distance was established. Second, it was perhaps the most dramatic finish in the history of the Olympic Games.

As a courtesy to King Edward VII and Queen Alexandra (great-grandparents of Queen Elizabeth II), Olympic officials broke precedent and agreed to hold the start of the race on the green lawns of Windsor Castle, which would serve as entertainment for the birthday party of one of their grandchildren. Olympic romanticists are bound to be shaken up when they find out that the Royal birthday present was the reason the marathon distance was established at 26 miles 385 yards — the actual distance from the start at Windsor Castle to the finish line in London's White City Stadium.

When the runners left the starting line there was nothing to indicate what would take place at the finish a little less than three hours later. London was experiencing a warm, muggy day and many of the pre-race favorites fell by the wayside, exhausted from the ordeal.

Throughout the race, the thousands in the stands had received reports sent ahead by motor car of the progress of the runners, but they were in the main dismayed, as several of the pre-race British favorites had been forced to leave the race. Now they were prepared to cheer on Charles Hefferon of South Africa, a member of the Commonwealth, who was battling for the lead with Italy's Dorando Pietri, a 22-year-old candy maker from Capri.

As Hefferon approached the stadium, he was faltering. America's 22-year-old Johnny Hayes passed him. Hayes was still 600 meters behind Pietri as the Italian entered the stadium.

Pietri entered the archway and it immediately became obvious he was in a state of collapse. He turned the wrong way and track officials rushed to him, turning him in the right direction. He ran a few yards, then collapsed in a heap. Spectators were shouting for officials to come to his aid, fearing for his life.

Dorando rose, ran a few steps and collapsed to the track again. Depending on which account is to be believed, Pietri rose and fell at least five times before crossing the finish line in the arms of one of the officials.

The Italian flag was raised on the victory pole as a surprisingly fresh Johnny Hayes entered the stadium and crossed the finish line.

Pietri was carried off the field on a stretcher and rumors spread through the stadium that he had died. Nevertheless, American officials protested that Pietri was illegally given assistance and should be disqualified. The protest was allowed and Johnny Hayes was declared the winner.

Pietri recovered quickly and became an international celebrity. His courage was rewarded by a sympathetic Queen Alexandra, who awarded him a special gold cup.

His fame spread to the United States where a young New York composer wrote a song, "Dorando, Dorando, Dorando." The composer's name was Irving Berlin.

A footnote to the story of Dorando was added by Joe Deakin, himself a gold medal winner in a relay at the 1908 London Games. In 1970, when he was 91, Deakin said he was a witness to the dramatic Pietri finish.

"The problem was that people along the roadway were giving him glasses of Chantilly instead of water," said Deakin. "Pietri wasn't exhausted. He was drunk."

Lis Hartel

Helsinki, 1952; Melbourne, 1956   Denmark

One of the least publicized or understood Olympic events is the 'dressage,' part of the equestrian competition.

Dressage, a non-jumping event, is judged when horse and rider go through a series of gaits and maneuvers without oral command. They appear as a single entity with the rider guiding the mount with hand and leg pressure all but invisible to the eye.

Dressage was first contested at the 1912 Stockholm Games and until 1952 was the most elite, snobbish and sexist event on the Olympic program. For 40 years dressage was open only to commissioned military officers. Non-commissioned officers, enlisted men, civilians and women were not eligible.

The 1952 Helsinki Games opened the event to everyone, but the main attraction was the four women competitors. One of them was 31-year-old Lis Hartel, one of the most revered athletes in Denmark's Olympic history.

In 1944, during World War II, 23-year-old Lis Hartel contracted polio during her pregnancy. Almost entirely paralyzed, she was determined to continue her career as one of Denmark's leading dressage riders.

While she was still pregnant, Lis Hartel began her rehabilitation. First, she struggled as she learned to lift her arms again, then regained use of her thigh muscles. Her daughter was born healthy, and Lis continued her comeback. First she began by crawling, then soon was able to walk haltingly with crutches. But she was not finished. She was determined to return to dressage competition.

"Why can't my horse be my legs?" she told those who doubted her quest.

Three years after her attack, in 1947, still unable to use her legs properly, she entered the Scandinavian Riding Championships and finished second. She continued to compete successfully and when the 1952 Olympics were scheduled for Helsinki, Lis Hartel was selected as one of Denmark's dressage competitors.

As one of the pioneer women in an event that was once exclusively male, Lis amazed the athletic world by winning the silver medal, even though she had to be assisted both on and off her horse.

The victory ceremony was one of the most emotional moments in all of Olympic history. The winner, Henry St. Cyr of Sweden, stood on the top step of the victory platform. When Lis Hartel's name was announced as the silver medal winner, St. Cyr stepped from the platform and assisted her to the second place position on the podium. The crowd cheered as Saint Cyr then returned to his position on the top step.

Four years later, Lis Hartel again won the silver medal in the dressage Olympic competition held in Stockholm. (The main Games were held in Melbourne but Australian quarantine regulations made it necessary to hold the equestrian events in Stockholm.) Again, as in Helsinki, Henry St. Cyr, the winner of the gold, assisted her to her position on the podium.

Lis Hartel had become a living example of a popular Danish saying:
"Life is not holding a good hand;
Life is playing a poor hand well."

Jackie Joyner-Kersee

Los Angeles, 1984; Seoul, 1988; Barcelona, 1992   United States

On September 23, 1988, 29 women prepared for the start of the seven-event heptathlon that would be contested over two days — four events the first day, three the second. To the winner would go to the title of "the finest all-around woman athlete in the world."

The heavy favorite to win the title was Jackie Joyner-Kersee of the United States, who had dominated the event in the two years leading to the Seoul Games. She had won the event nationally and internationally nine straight times. In addition she scored more than 7,000 points on four different occasions, a barrier once considered unreachable. No other woman had ever approached this mark. Her greatness becomes even more enhanced with the recognition that Joyner-Kersee suffers from exercise-induced asthma.

Ironically, Joyner-Kersee's last loss was four years earlier at the 1984 Los Angeles Games. Then she was leading after six events with only the 800 meters left. But she was totally exhausted and ran one of the poorest races of her career. When the final points were tabulated, Joyner-Kersee had to settle for the silver medal, five points behind the winner, Glynis Nunn of Australia. Afterward Joyner-Kersee learned that if she had leaped three centimeters farther in the long jump or run the 800 meters one third of a second faster, the gold medal would have been hers. After the Los Angeles Games, Jackie married her coach, Bob Kersee, and together they worked toward the Seoul Olympics and the possibility of two gold medals — the heptathlon and her favorite event, the long jump.

"We don't take the practice sessions home very often," said Bob Kersee with a smile. "And when I'm on the field with Jackie, she's my athlete, not my wife. . . I'm going to coach her just like I coach everybody else."

"It's true," said Jackie. "On the field it's coach-athlete with me and Bobby. But when we get home if I don't agree with him I let him know about it."

In the heptathlon's 100 meter hurdles, the first event at the 1988 Seoul Games, Jackie was by far the best. She went into the lead and was four points better than her own world record pace which she had established at the Olympic trials. In the second event, the high jump, she strained her left knee. Nevertheless, she retained her overall lead, but had fallen 87 points behind her world record. With her leg heavily taped, she got off her second longest throw ever in the shot-put, but she was still well behind her world record. In the final event of the first day, the 200 meter dash, Jackie was the fastest of all the competitors, but she nevertheless was more than 100 points off her world mark.

"I was scared after the first day," recalled Jackie. "I was afraid my leg might stiffen overnight. I wasn't thinking world record. I just wanted the gold."

The long jump, her favorite, was the first event of the second day. Quickly she realized her fears had been for naught. . . she leaped brilliantly, best of all the competitors, and had pulled up to within eleven points of her world record. Jackie was mediocre in the javelin. She lost considerable points toward the world record but easily maintained her overall lead.

"I was scared when I went to the line for the last event, the 800 meters," said Jackie. "So I said to myself, just don't get caught up with the fast pace I know the East Europeans are going to run. Just run my own race. The gold medal is mine, the world record can wait."

"I had another idea," said Bob Kersee. "I knew if she kept close so the East Europeans she could get her record."

During the first lap of the two-lap race, Jackie was in fifth place. She was feeling good. She was within striking distance of the East Europeans and wasn't feeling the exhaustion she suffered four years before.

As she came down the homestretch, Bob Kersee was cheering her on.

"Go Jackie. . . Go Jackie. . . Go Jackie. . ." he screamed as she crossed the finish line. Then he leaped over the fence to the track and embraced her, screaming, "You got the world record, you got the world record."

Jackie had run her second fastest 800 meters ever to break her own world record by 76 points.

Four days after her momentous heptathlon victory, Jackie added new glory in the long jump. On her fifth attempt she broke the Olympic record and with it won her second gold medal in Seoul.

Four years later in Barcelona, she repeated her heptathlon victory and won the silver in the long jump.

29

Pablo Morales

Los Angeles, 1984; Barcelona, 1992   United States

On July 27, 1992, at the Olympic swim stadium in Barcelona, eight finalists prepared for the start of the 100 meter butterfly, one of the most eagerly awaited events of the swimming competition — the meeting between defending Olympic champion Anthony Nesty of Surinam and 27-year-old Pablo Morales of the United States.

Nesty won the event four years earlier in Seoul but Morales has held the world record for more than six years. Morales' career has been filled with tragedy. Eight years earlier when he was nineteen, he was the favorite to win both the 100 meter and 200 meter butterfly events at the 1984 Los Angeles Olympics. But he failed miserably, finishing second to the world record setting winner, Michael Gross of West Germany, and then coming in fourth in the 200 meter butterfly.

Though Morales won another silver medal in the 200 meter individual medley and a gold as a member of the 400 meter medley team, his performances were not as predicted. Before the Games many thought he had a good opportunity to win four gold medals.

Unbelievably, however, Morales failed in the 1988 Olympic trials, unable to make the team when he finished third in both the 100 and 200 meter butterfly. "I was terribly disappointed," recalled Morales, "Between Seoul and the Barcelona Games I ate, dreamt and slept swimming. I believed that winning in Barcelona would be the natural conclusion to my swimming career.

"I was devastated after those losses," continues Morales. "At the time I believed I would never get back to competitive swimming again. I set my mind on attending Cornell Law School. Around the second year of law school, I started contemplating the idea of coming back. My mom was terribly sick with cancer and after she died I made my decision. I told the people at law school that I was taking a year off and started to train again for Barcelona."

On March 2, 1992, six months after his comeback, Morales made it to the United States Olympic trials in Indianapolis. His father, Pedro, watched from the stands.

"I was there with my daughter," said Pedro Morales. "I asked my daughter whether she had brought a picture of Mom. She took it out of her purse and handed it to me. I held it up during the entire race so that she would be watching Pablo."

Incredibly, Morales won his race. After eight years he had again made the Olympic team.

"For years I had been waiting for this moment," said Morales. "Being at the starting line in the Olympic final with the world champion Anthony Nesty next to me. And finally it happened."

Morales got off quickly in the Olympic final.

"My plan was to establish an early lead," said Morales. "Nesty has an incredible finish and I wanted to have enough of a lead to hold him off."

At 75 meters Morales still led, but Nesty in fourth was starting his final kick.

"I could feel Nesty coming on," recalled Morales. "On the other side of me was Rafal Szukala of Poland, who was also making a charge. I concentrated on the wall and as it got closer I just stretched my arms out to the wall. I looked at the scoreboard and my name was up there first."

Morales had won the gold medal followed by Poland's Szukala in second and Anthony Nesty of Surinam, third.

"There was a lot of emotion for me on the victory platform," said Morales. "Hearing the national anthem, my thoughts turned to my mother. We had shared so much together when I was growing up. . . watching the Olympic Games on television together, and she nodding when I told her one day I would win an Olympic gold medal. And now that my time had finally come. . . and she couldn't be there in person. . . nevertheless I felt that she was smiling with approval from above."

1936 Women's Relay Berlin, 1936

August 9, 1936, the last day of the track and field competition at the Berlin Olympic Games, had all the earmarks of being a momentous day for Chancellor Adolf Hitler and a host of Nazi dignitaries who arrived early at the Olympic stadium.

The Nazi hierarchy, along with 80,000 spectators, mostly German, were there to witness what was predicted to be the most certain gold medal performance of the entire track and field competition — the victory of their magnificent 4 x 100 women's relay team.

Up to this point German women had been making Propaganda Minister Joseph Goebbels' pronouncements look good — that the Nazi system bred superior athletes. German women had earlier won gold medals in the discus and javelin and now the stage was set for them to win their first gold medal in a running event at the 1936 Games — the 4 x 100 relay.

Three of the four relay members, Kathe Krauss, Marie Dollinger and Emmy Albus, had finished 3rd, 4th and 6th in the 100 meters behind America's Helen Stephens, the gold medal winner a few days before. What raised eyebrows, however, was their anchor leg Ilse Dorffeldt, the lone German relay member who hadn't competed in the 100 meter dash.

The German women were loaded with speed. They had broken the world record in their semi-final heat the day before and by comparative times none of the other five teams in the finals was within seven meters of them.

The lone threat to the Germans was the American foursome anchored by Helen Stephens. . . . The American team won their semi-final heat in a time that was seven-tenths of a second slower than the newly set German world record. But in relay racing seven-tenths is the equivalent of close to seven meters.

The arrow at the bottom right indicates the fallen baton which slipped from the grasps of teammates Marie Dollinger and

For the final the German race strategy was quite simple. They would build up an overwhelming lead over the first three legs so that even a magnificent closing effort by Helen Stephens would still leave the Americans far behind.

If the race went as planned, Ilse Dorffeldt would take the baton for the final leg with a ten meter lead. Then if America's Stephens ran her fastest time ever, Ilse Dorffeldt would still be able to cross the finish line at least three meters in front.

For three quarters of the race the German team ran as predicted. Emmy Albus, their leadoff runner, gave them a three meter lead. Kathe Krauss added another three meters and their third runner, Marie Dollinger, gave them an additional four meters. As Ilse Dorffeldt waited for the final passoff, Germany was ten meters in front, too much for Helen Stephens to make up.

Then tragedy struck the German team. It is doubtful if anyone in the stadium saw exactly what happened. The first clue to the disaster came when Ilse Dorffeldt, as if struck by an assassin's bullet, grabbed her head with both hands, her face contorted in anguish. Ilse Dorffeldt had dropped the baton. America's Helen Stephens raced to the finish to win the gold medal.

The three other German runners raced to Dorffeldt to console her while the American team joyfully mobbed the victorious Stephens.

"We were in shock until the next day," remembered Emmy Albus more than a half century later. "I know this sounds strange but Hitler was very sympathetic. The next day he sent us all flowers." Helen Stephens, who died in 1994, discounted the German tragedy. Throughout her life, she maintained, "I would have won the race even if they hadn't dropped the baton."

Ilse Dorffeldt, losing an almost certain gold medal for Germany.

Takeichi Nishi
Los Angeles, 1932

Japan

The individual equestrian jumping competition, the Prix Des Nations, has been on the Olympic program since the 1900 Games in Paris. It is a contest where horse and rider travel over a course of obstacles of various heights with single, double and triple fences. The event consists of two rounds and the winner at the end is the rider with the least "faults." Faults are assessed for knocking down an obstacle or exceeding the time limit around the course.

A story that had a poignant climax in 1945 began thirteen years earlier in Los Angeles in the Prix Des Nations Olympic competition.

One of the most popular athletes at the Games was Lieutenant Takeichi Nishi of Japan. He was born into a Royal Japanese family and beside his military rank, could also be addressed as Baron Nishi.

In the weeks preceding the Los Angeles Games, the debonair Army lieutenant was the toast of the Hollywood social scene. He became close friends with the legendary motion picture stars of the day — Will Rogers, Charlie Chaplin, Mary Pickford and Douglas Fairbanks, to name a few.

Nishi spoke perfect English and his appearance at the many pre-Olympic parties brought his photograph to the society section more often than it appeared on the sports pages.

His popularity was such that the thousands watching the Prix Des Nations cheered him as much as they did the Americans in the competition.

It was therefore no surprise that he received a huge ovation when he, with his mount, Uranus, completed the two rounds with but eight faults — giving him the gold medal. The crowd roared as if an American had won.

Nishi kept on corresponding with his motion picture friends after returning home. This relationship continued until December 7, 1941 — the Japanese attack on Pearl Harbor.

Nishi rose quickly through the ranks and finally, as a colonel, commanded a tank battalion in the bloody battle of Iwo Jima. After weeks of fighting, his troops were finally cornered inside massive caves with no hope of survival short of surrender. With orders to "fight to the finish," Nishi stayed with his troops and with them committed suicide. He was one of the thousands of soldiers on both sides who lost their lives in what many describe as the bloodiest battle of the Pacific War.

When peace was declared, his motion picture friends said their final farewells. A wreath was sent to the spot where he died, inscribed with the words, "To our dear friend, Baron Nishi, with whom we spent so many joyous days."

The charismatic Nishi is second from the right in this photo of the Japanese equestrian team.

Milt Campbell

Helsinki, 1952; Melbourne, 1956   United States

Recently Milt Campbell was inducted into the International Swimming Hall of Fame. In high school Milt was an All–State fullback on the football team and an outstanding hurdler in track and field. Arguably he was America's greatest all-around Olympic athlete who competed as a decathlete in two Olympics, finishing second to Bob Mathias as an eighteen-year-old in Helsinki in 1952, and winning the gold medal four

years later in Melbourne, defeating his teammate, the legendary Rafer Johnson. Yet today, Milt Campbell remains one of the least known and heralded of all the men who have earned the title as "the greatest all-around athlete in the world."

Though he won his first decathlon championship in 1953 in the AAU Championships, Campbell concentrated on the 110 meter hurdles as his best chance of winning a gold medal at the 1956 Melbourne Olympics.

However, he finished fourth in the Olympic trials and failed to qualify. He then decided to try the decathlon again. Most experts predicted that he would be most fortunate to win the silver behind his teammate Rafer Johnson.

Johnson had defeated him in the Olympic trials, but it was a different Milt Campbell he would be facing at the Melbourne Games.

Campbell started off superbly, winning the first event, the 100 meters. The victory was no fluke. At the end of the first five events, Campbell led Johnson by 189 points.

The first event on the second day was the 110 meter hurdles, Campbell's best event. As expected, Campbell, the future world record holder, sped down the course in fourteen seconds flat, defeating Johnson by more than a second. With four events left, only a total collapse would deprive him of the gold medal. Though Johnson was competing with a slight injury, it is doubtful that, even in perfect physical shape, he would have defeated Campbell this day.

Campbell had a chance at breaking Johnson's world record, but in the eighth event, the pole vault, his best leap was almost a foot less than his previous top mark. He lost valuable points in his quest for Johnson's world record.

As the tenth event got under way, the 1,500 meter run, the gold medal was his, but the most dramatic moments of the competition were yet to come.

"As we were going into the last lap, the Russian Kuznyetsov was in front and I was behind him," remembered Campbell. "I was content to stay behind him, but then I heard this voice off my shoulder behind me saying, 'Come on, big boy. It's time to run. You can do better than this.'

"I looked and saw that it was Ian Bruce of Australia, who wasn't even in the top ten. And he kept yelling at me: 'Come on, pick it up. . . pick it up. . . stay in there with me. . . come on boy. . . you can do it.' So he started to sprint and I started to sprint with him. I couldn't believe it. Here's a guy whom I never met urging me on. I stayed with him and incredibly we passed the Russian and now Bruce and I were racing to the finish. At the line he just nipped me out. . . but I'll never forget him. They can talk about the true Olympic spirit and laugh at it. But Ian Bruce showed me it does exist."

37

Oksana Baiul
Lillehammer, 1994

The dramatic story of sixteen-year-old Oksana Baiul of Ukraine reached its climax on the evening of February 25, 1994, when the women's free skating final at the Lillehammer Olympics was scheduled.

Baiul was in second place within striking distance of the leader, America's Nancy Kerrigan. However, Baiul's physical condition for this final competition was suspect. The day before, Oksana collided with another skater during a practice session and suffered injuries to her back and leg. The leg injury required three stitches. The pain was severe enough for Oksana to ask for and get approval from the IOC to receive painkilling injections.

The accident was a continuation of the tragedies Oksana had to endure in her young life. She never knew her father, who left home when she was a small child. Her mother died of cancer when she was thirteen, followed by the death of her grandparents with whom she then lived. When she was fourteen, her coach of nine years emigrated to Canada. Oksana was all but alone.

Into her life at this time came skater Viktor Petrenko, the 1992 Albertville gold medal winner. Petrenko was coached by his mother-in-law, Galina Zmievskaya.

"My son-in-law Viktor Petrenko came to me and asked me if I would take Oksana into my home," recalled Zmievskaya. "He had been giving her money for costumes and food. Viktor said to me, 'She is such a small girl, how much can she cost, how much can she eat?' So she became a member of my family and I became her coach."

By the luck of the draw, Nancy Kerrigan, the leader, would skate before Oksana. Kerrigan performed brilliantly and to many gave a gold medal performance. Win or lose, she had silenced her critics who questioned her ability to perform under extreme pressure. Nevertheless, there was still room for Baiul to win the gold medal. "I knew the first jump was the most critical," said Zmievskaya. "We did not know whether her leg would hold up on the landing because of the injections." Baiul's first jump was spectacular — a triple lutz, the first of five triple jumps she would perform.

"I was praying to God she would have enough strength to finish the program," said Zmievskaya. "I think Oksana and I were the only ones who knew what she was going through."

When Oksana finished her routine, the crowd responded with a thunderous ovation. Now she had to wait for the scores to be announced. The final tabulations were almost impossible to comprehend. Of the nine judges four gave their first place votes to Baiul and four to Kerrigan.

The ninth judge, from Germany, called it a tie. But by the rules of the competition ties are broken by the skater with the highest artistic score. Though the German judge gave Kerrigan the higher score for technical merit, he gave Oksana a tenth of a point higher in the artistic category. Baiul was the gold medal winner with five first place votes to four for Nancy Kerrigan.

Standing on the victory platform, Oksana's thoughts turned to Viktor and Galina. The words: "To achieve great things in life, with the help of others, one can overcome the sadness of the past."

There was one more honor for Oksana Baiul. Because of her, for the first time in Olympic history the Ukrainian national anthem was played.

1956 Yale Crew Melbourne, 1956

The eight oar crew race, a classic event on the Olympic rowing program, has been contested since the 1900 Games in Paris. Leading to the Melbourne Games of 1956, American crews had won nine of the eleven gold medals. Great Britain won the other two.

At the 1956 Melbourne Games the American crew faced an even more formidable record: to continue a consecutive win streak that was 36 years old. Since the 1920 victory in Antwerp, American "eights" had won seven successive gold medals and never lost a single heat. The United States was represented by the Yale University championship crew team.

On the second day of the Melbourne Olympics, this unblemished string was broken. In their qualifying heat, the United States finished third behind Australia and Canada. Only the first two finishers go on to the next round.

The United States would now have to win the "repechage," the race that gives another opportunity for all the teams that failed to qualify in their heats to stay in the competition. It is known as "the race of losers" and the winner goes on to the semi-final. However, never in history had any team won the gold medal after losing its opening race.

"It was a real shock," remembered John Cooke, one of the American crew members. "We knew about the Canadians but not much about the Australians. We were gaining at the end but it wasn't enough."

Two days later, the United States faced Italy, Great Britain and France in the repechage, the

four teams who failed to qualify in their opening round.

"We were not taking any chances this time," remembered Cooke. "We won the race very handily. We got some of our confidence back but we couldn't be too cocky. We had beaten a bunch of losers."

The victory put the Americans in the semi-final where they would have to face the Australians again, one of the teams that defeated them in the opening round.

"We had to prove to ourselves that we could beat the Australians," remembered Cooke, "even though the first two finishers would get into the final. Both Australia and our team easily outdistanced the other two crews, so that it was no contest. First or second didn't matter to the Australians but it mattered to us. We rowed all out like it was the final. With about 300 meters left, the Australian coxswain yelled out, "Ease off, Yanks, you've got it, ease off."

The Americans won the semi–final. The Australian press criticized the Americans for their "ego trip," and predicted this "silly" effort would hurt them in the final. "We didn't care about the criticism," said Cooke. "It was a psychological boost."

On November 27, 1956, the United States lined up against Australia, Sweden and Canada for the final over the 2,000 meter course. The United States trailed until there were 500 meters left. Then, rowing at an incredible clip, 40 strokes to the minute, the United States edged ahead.

"We're going to win it. We're going to win it!" screamed coxswain Bill Becklean.

The Americans crossed the finish line the winner, followed by Canada, Australia and Sweden. The United States had created Olympic history — the first team ever to win the gold medal after an opening round defeat.

"I was so tired, my teammates had to help me out of the boat," recalled Cooke. "Somehow, they got me to the victory podium. Then I collapsed and they had to cart me off to the hospital."

Far left: The Australian eight oar crew, which provided opposition to the American team both in and out of the water. Left: The American crew; John Cooke is third from right. In background: Nearing the end of the eight oar crew final, the United States (top) forges ahead of Australia (third place) and Canada (second place).

Bob Beamon
Mexico City, 1968   United States

At the 1968 Mexico City Olympics Bob Beamon was in danger of being eliminated from the long jump in the qualification round. His first two attempts were fouls. One more botched attempt and he would be going home that day.

His friend and teammate, Ralph Boston, came over to help him. "It was like Jesse Owens and Luz Long all over again," recalled Beamon, remembering the scene more than a quarter of a century later.

"Luz Long came to Jesse's aid at the 1936 Berlin Olympics after Jesse fouled in his first two qualifying attempts. Ralph Boston did the same for me. He told me, 'Bob, you won't foul if you take off a foot behind the foul line. You can't miss.' Basically that's what Luz Long told Jesse and I took Ralph's advice. I qualified."

Later in the afternoon, the long jump final coincided with the final of the 400 meters. America's Lee Evans, who won the gold medal, recalled a funny incident.

"The eight finalists for the 400 meters were walking onto the field," smiled Evans, "and the public address announcer was calling out the competitors. When he announced my name, the crowd let out an incredible roar and that made me happy. I never realized that so many people were pulling for me. Actually, they were cheering for something that took place at the

long jump pit. Then I looked across the field and saw officials and athletes running all over the place, and Bob was jumping up and down, then kneeling, holding his hands to his head. I didn't know what was happening."

"Neither did I," laughed Beamon these many years later. "I knew I made a great jump and I heard some of the guys saying things like 8.9 meters . . . or something. Outside the United States everything is in meters, so I wasn't

sure how far I had jumped. I knew it was more than 27 feet 4 3/4 inches, which was the world record. Then Ralph Boston came over and said, 'Bob, I think it's over 29 feet,' which was almost 2 feet farther than the world record. Then I said to Ralph, 'What happened to 28 feet?'

After many minutes, the public address system announced the history-making news. "Bob Beamon's leap, 8.90 meters. . . 29 feet 2½ inches." The crowd roared, some questioning whether they heard correctly. It soon became official.

The rest of the competitors were in shock. For all practical purposes the competition was over in the first round.

Christa Rothenburger-Luding

At 5:00 p.m., Saturday, September 24, 1988, at the Seoul Olympic velodrome, thousands in the stands anticipated one of the historic moments at the Olympics — the final competition of the women's cycling 1,000 meter sprint, the first time it was on the Olympic program.

After three days of competition, two women remained: 26-year-old Erika Salumae of the Soviet Union, the 1987 world champion, and 28-year-old Christa Rothenburger-Luding of the German Democratic Republic, the world champion in 1986.

For Christa Rothenburger-Luding, there was an opportunity to create Olympic history — to become the first woman to win gold medals in both the winter and summer Games.

Until then Eddie Eagan of the United States was the only athlete to complete such a feat. At the 1920 Antwerp

Games Eagan won the light-heavyweight boxing gold medal. Twelve years later, at the 1932 Lake Placid Olympics, Eagan was a member of the United States' victorious four-man bobsled team.

But here in Seoul, Rothenburger-Luding had a chance not only to equal his record but in a sense, to surpass it. If she won, she would have done it in the *same* Olympic year and in *individual* rather than team events.

Seven months earlier at the Calgary Winter Olympics, Christa came down the homestretch to win the 1,000 meter speed skating gold medal, to go with the 500 meter gold she won at the 1984 Sarajevo Games.

Christa married her longtime coach, Ernst Luding, two months after the Calgary Games. He was instrumental in making her a winter-summer athlete.

"We decided that Christa should train in cycling to

bridge the gap between the two seasons. . . winter and summer," said Ernst Luding. "She has the same special qualities for cycling as she does for speed skating. . . strength and speed."

Here at the Seoul Olympics both Salumae and Rothenburger-Luding had each won three races leading to the final. Now they would face each other in the best two out of three races for the gold medal. Rothenburger-Luding won the first heat, but Salumae immediately came back to defeat her in the second.

As always, cycling sprint races are a combination of tactics and speed. Going into the final 200 meters to the finish, most cyclists prefer the trailing position. Then they can conserve energy and draft off the leader. At world class level, the key to victory is to choose the precise moment of surprise and energy that will catapult the trailing rider to victory.

With 200 meters left in this final race, Salumae trailed Rothenburger-Luding. They were again playing "cat and mouse." Finally, Salumae made her move. Rothenburger-Luding stayed with her. They were even, wheel to wheel, as the finish line approached. Finally, Salumiae edged ahead and won the gold medal.

"It was so close," remembered Rothenburger-Luding. "After the final race I talked with my husband Ernst. We both agreed that the difference was only six inches at the finish."

Her husband was more philosophical. "There's a saying we have in Germany," smiled Ernst Luding, "that shared pain is half pain. She has stood on the top step of the victory podium at the Winter Games and the second highest step in the Summer Games. . . so with the sorrow there is so much joy we can share."

Károly Takács

London, 1948; Helsinki, 1952   Hungary

In 1938 Sergeant Károly Takács of the Hungarian Army was one of the finest rapid fire pistol shooters in the world. He was a member of the world championship Hungarian team that was expected to dominate the upcoming 1940 Olympic Games scheduled for Tokyo.

One day on military maneuvers with his squad, a terrible accident occurred. A defective pin exploded a hand grenade in Takács' right hand before he could toss it. His right hand was blown off.

"I spent a month in the hospital and was very depressed," said Takács. "As soon as I left the hospital I made a decision. Why not try the left hand?"

"I practiced all the time by myself," said Takács. "So no one knew what I was doing. Finally, in the spring of 1939, I decided to go to my country's pistol shooting championship. The shooters all came over to me and told me how sorry they were about my accident and how proud they were that I came to watch them shoot. I told them, 'I didn't come to watch you, I came to compete.' They were even more surprised when I won."

World War II canceled the 1940 and 1944 Olympics, and it appeared that Takács' hopes of ever winning a gold medal were dashed.

Because of his national fame as a pistol shooter, his disability was waived by the Hungarian Army and he was permitted to remain in service during the war. He continued to practice with his left hand. By the end of the conflict Takács was raised in rank to captain.

When the Games were revived in London in 1948, Captain Károly Takács made the Hungarian team. A day before the rapid fire pistol shooting championship he was introduced to 1947 world champion Carlos Valiente of Argentina, the favorite to win the gold medal.

"Valiente was very surprised to see me," laughed Takács. "He thought my career was over. He asked me why I was in London. I told him, 'I'm here to learn.' He looked at me quite strangely."

In London at the age of 38, Takács won the gold medal, breaking Valiente's world record by ten points.

"Valiente won the silver medal," recalled Takács with a smile. "And on the victory platform he congratulated me. Then he said, 'Captain Takács, you have learned enough.'"

Four years later in Helsinki, Captain Takács again won the gold medal, defeating his countryman Szilárd Kun by one point. Carlos Valiente finished fourth by two points. After the victory ceremony, Valiente again came over to Takács and remembered the previous conversation. "You have learned too much," Valiente said, smiling. "Now it is time for you to retire and teach me."

There were great celebrations for Captain Takács when he returned to Budapest after the 1952 Olympics.

"Everybody was giving me things except for the thing I wanted most," laughed Takács. "So I gave myself a present. No, I gave myself three presents. I had three right hands made especially for skiing, swimming and boxing."

47

Despite a broken kneecap, Shun Fujimoto, second from right, was able to make a significant contribution to his team's gold medal performance.

Shun Fujimoto Montreal, 1976

In the gymnastic competition at the 1932 Los Angeles Olympic Games, the Japanese team finished last in the standings. The defeat was humiliating. They vowed to become a gymnastic power.

After World War II, the Japanese fulfilled their pledge. Their individual champions vied with the Soviet Union for world supremacy.

One of the most prestigious gymnastic titles at the Olympics is the team championship. Leading to the 1976 Montreal Games, the Japanese team had defeated the Soviet Union in Olympic competition four times and won the team title: Rome, Tokyo, Mexico City and Munich. In Montreal, 1976, they were going after their fifth straight team gold medal. Again, their main opposition was the male gymnasts of the Soviet Union.

Each team is permitted six entrants but only the five highest scores of the members are counted in the final tabulation. During the competition a severe blow was suffered by the Japanese. One of their star competitors, Shun Fujimoto, broke his kneecap while performing the floor exercise.

Olympic rules prevented him from using a painkiller. He decided to continue in the competition and try to endure the pain. "I did not want to worry my teammates," recalled Fujimoto. "The competition was so close I didn't want them to lose their concentration with worry about me."

His next event was the side horse. Without letting his coaches or teammates know of his injury, Fujimoto performed the exercise well, receiving a 9.5 out of a possible 10.

His next event would be crucial — the rings. This event tests the arm strength of the gymnast and vital points can be won or lost on landing at the end of the performance. Amazingly, Fujimoto impressed the judges with his strength and skill. Only the dismount remained. He would have to land after a swinging routine that would propel him to the ground with great velocity.

"I knew when I descended from the rings, it would be the most painful moment. I also knew that if my posture was not good when I landed I would not receive a good score. I must try to forget the pain," recalled Fujimoto.

When Fujimoto landed, he smiled for the judges, held his position for an appropriate amount of time, then his leg buckled beneath. Incredibly, the judges awarded him a 9.7.

But now the pain was excruciating, for the landing had aggravated his injury further. Fujimoto wanted to continue but Japanese officials and his teammates would have none of it. He was not permitted to stay in the competition.

Knowing they must perform impeccably with only their remaining five members, the Japanese team was inspired to greater heights. They knew that each one of them could not make a major mistake.

A few hours later the final tabulation for the team championship was announced. The Japanese gymnasts won the title for the fifth consecutive time and dedicated their victory to their fallen teammate, Shun Fujimoto. The margin of victory was forty-hundredths of a point.

László Papp

László Papp of Hungary is perhaps the most unknown "legend" in Olympic boxing history. In a sport which has seen such familiar names as Floyd Patterson, Muhammad Ali, Joe Frazier, George Foreman and Sugar Ray Leonard springboard their Olympic gold medals into professional world championship titles, László never had the opportunity to really show his prowess outside the Olympic arena.

At the 1948 London Games, Papp fought as a middleweight and easily won the gold medal. "I began boxing during the Second World War in 1944," said Papp. "Before winning my gold medal in London I had 51 amateur bouts and lost only one. Forty-seven of my victories were by knockouts. Nevertheless, in London nobody knew who I was until I won the gold medal."

Four years later in Helsinki, Papp decided to go down in weight and entered the light-middleweight division. Again, he went through the five-bout competition without a defeat, scoring two of his victories by knockouts.

"It was difficult to train in Hungary during this time," recalls Papp. "I think having a job helped me gain strength. Every day I had to carry large, heavy packages up and down stairs. So I guess you might say I had strength training every day for my arms and legs."

With two gold medals under his belt when the 1956 Melbourne Games approached, Papp, now 30, decided to try for the third time.

Just before the Hungarian team was to leave for Melbourne, Soviet troops moved into Budapest to suppress the internal revolution.

"The country was in turmoil," Papp said. "Many of the athletes wished to abandon the competition and stay home. We were all saddened because of so much killing and bloodshed. However, I thought I could do best for my country and compete. I am not a Communist. I am a Catholic and a very religious man. My church, my religion, my country are very important to me."

In Melbourne Papp easily moved through the competition. In the light-middleweight final he would face José Torres of the United States, who nine years later would become light-heavyweight champion of the world.

In a close fight, Papp was awarded the decision and his third gold medal.

"I was praying I won the gold medal," recalled Torres. "It was such a close fight. . . the toughest fight I ever had. When they announced that he won the decision, I was not disappointed. It could have gone either way and he was a great champion."

At the time Papp created Olympic history — the first boxer ever to win three gold medals. One year after the Melbourne Games, 31-year-old László Papp scored another first. He became the first athlete from a Communist country to receive permission to turn professional.

Papp had 30 professional fights without a defeat, but never fought for a world championship. At the age of 38 he retired and began training young Hungarian boxers for future Olympic Games.

Fanny Blankers-Koen London, 1948

Babe Didrikson and Jackie Joyner-Kersee are the two names most mentioned whenever the "greatest" all-around woman athlete is discussed. Arguably, there is a third woman whom many place above the other two. Her name is Fanny Blankers-Koen of Holland. As an eighteen-year-old at the 1936 Berlin Olympics, the then Fanny Koen showed little to indicate her subsequent greatness. She finished sixth in the high jump and ran the second leg on the 4 x 100 Dutch relay team that finished fifth.

After the Games, Fanny married her coach Jan Blankers and looked forward to competing in the 1940 Olympics, but they were canceled because of World War II. With Holland occupied by the Germans during the war, Fanny continued to train even though she was now the mother of two small children.

When the Games were renewed in London in 1948, Fanny shocked the Dutch sporting community by announcing she would compete in four events—the 100 and 200 meters, the 80 meter hurdles and the 4 x 100 meter relay. Ironically, she was the world record holder in the long jump and high jump, but those events conflicted with the other running events. Fanny chose to enter only the running events.

Dutch newspapers wrote painfully negative stories about her attempt. In England, a British Olympic official named Jack Crump was quoted as saying, "Why is a 30-year-old mother of two running in short pants at the expense of leaving her family?" Fanny's reply was simple. "I will show him," she said in anger toward her friend, and main accuser, Jack Crump.

And show them she did. Fanny won the 100 meters and two days later ran the 80 meter hurdles. The race was a close one between Fanny and Maureen Gardner of Great Britain and the decision was not easily determined. As the runners waited for the results, Fanny suddenly became confused.

"Without warning, the band began to play 'God Save the King,'" remembered Fanny with a smile, and the predominately British crowd roared their acclaim. "I remembered that they play the national anthem for the winning athlete, so I thought Maureen Gardner had won. Then they announced that King George VI had just arrived at the stadium and they were playing the English national anthem for him." A few minutes later Fanny was announced the winner of the hurdles by one foot.

"Even though I had won the two

Blankers-Koen receives her gold medal for the 200 meters while second place Williamson (Britain) and third place Patterson (U.S.A.) look on.

gold medals," she recalled, "I was very depressed. The press would not stop questioning me, and I got even sadder after talking to my children in Amsterdam who said they missed me. So I told my husband I would not compete anymore and would go home."

Coach Blankers watched Fanny weeping inconsolably at her decision and waited for her to compose herself. "I understand that you have done what you said you would do," he told her. "But if you stay and compete and win the 200 meters and the relay, you will do what no other woman has ever done in track and field — win four gold medals. And also remember that only Jesse Owens has done this before." Jan Blankers knew what he was doing. Owens had been Fanny's idol.

"OK, I'll stay. I'll call the children and tell them they must wait," said Fanny.

She then went on to win gold medals in the 200 meters and relay and to this day is the only woman to perform such a feat in track and field. Many believe that if she had entered the long jump and high jump, she could have won six gold medals.

Fanny returned to Amsterdam to a hero's welcome. A national holiday was declared and Fanny, Jan and their two children were paraded in a horse-drawn carriage throughout the city before thousands of her countrymen. It was reported that the celebration was greater than the one on V-E day when Holland was liberated from the Nazis.

Her British friend, Jack Crump, wrote an apology to Fanny, which she happily accepted. But perhaps the most poignant words ended a news story of her great triumphs. "Holland has won four gold medals in Olympic track and field history . . . and Fanny has won them all. . . ."

53

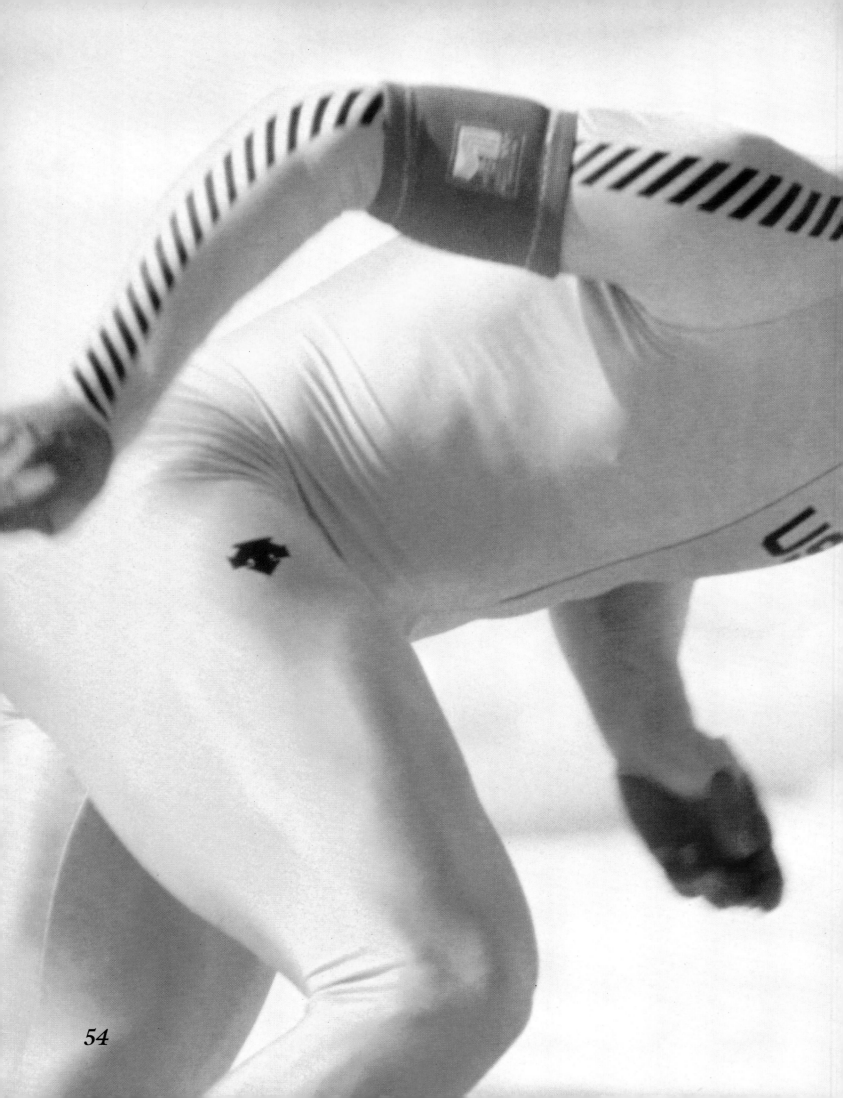

54

Eric Heiden Lake Placid, 1980

There is a vast difference in speed skating between the sprinters and long distance competitors. Sprinters usually compete in the 500 and 1,000 meters and the distance experts in the 5,000 and 10,000 meters. The fifth event, the 1,500 meters, is usually "no man's land" — too long for the sprinters and too short for the long distance specialists.

As the 1980 Lake Placid Olympics approached, Eric Heiden of the United States was poised to upset the sprinter-distance beliefs. He was entered in all five races and many believed he had a chance to win all five.

An indication of things to come took place in the 500 meters, Heiden's first event. He was in the first pairing and his opponent was the world record holder, Yevgeny Kulikov of the Soviet Union. To many, Heiden's extravagant quest appeared over after 100 meters of the 500 meter race. Kulikov was ahead by five-hundredths of a second. . . . But in a thrilling finish, Heiden was inches ahead.

The next day in the 5,000 meters, after one third of his race, Heiden was almost five seconds behind a Norwegian skater, Tom Erik Oxholm, who had gone before him.

But as in the 500, he finished strong at the end for his second successive gold medal.

Heiden's third race was the 1,000 meters. Heiden won by a second and a half — an incredible distance in a world class sprint race.

Two days later Heiden continued his remarkable streak by winning the 1,500 meters by more than a second. The margin was even more spectacular, for he slipped on a turn at the 600 meter mark, losing valuable parts of a second.

On the final day of the men's skating competition, the 10,000 meters was scheduled. The night before, rather than rest, Heiden was one of the screaming spectators urging on the United States hockey team, who defeated the heavily favored Soviet Union, a prelude to their winning the hockey gold medal.

The next morning Heiden demolished the opposition — breaking the old world record by more than six seconds. Even more formidable was the fact that the second place finisher was almost eight seconds behind him.

Eric Heiden had performed a feat unprecedented in the annals of speed skating — five gold medals in five events.

Though Mark Spitz won seven gold medals in seven swimming events at the 1972 Munich Games, Heiden's performance is considered greater. Heiden won all his races in individual events, while Spitz's momentous feat was attained in four individual events and as part of three relay teams.

Joseph Guillemot

Antwerp, 1920   France ▮▮

On August 17, 1920, sixteen men lined up for the final of the 5,000 meter run at the Antwerp Olympic Games. The race was the long anticipated debut of 23-year-old Paavo Nurmi of Finland. Also at the starting line was 20-year-old Joseph Guillemot of France, whose main claim to fame was that he was still alive.

More than two years earlier, when he was in combat on the Western front against the Germans in World War I, Guillemot was a victim of a poison gas attack that left his lungs severely burned. Once it was determined that he would live, doctors were uncertain as to how to treat him.

Finally it was decided they would try a revolutionary regimen for Guillemot — a training program of easy jogging and long distance running. The hope was that deep breathing and exercise could be beneficial in the healing of his lungs.

No one can explain the complete recovery of Joseph Guillemot. By the time the war was over he had returned to active duty, and when peace was declared, Guillemot, the "miracle soldier," was competing in actual running races.

After one of his improbable victories in a 5,000 meter race the year before the 1920 Antwerp Olympics, Guillemot was given a complete physical examination. The result was that Guillemot had a body that defied convention and the scars from his poison gas attack during the war were no longer a problem for him. The French Athletic Association then made a momentous decision. Joseph Guillemot would represent them in the 5,000 and 10,000 meters at the 1920 Antwerp Olympics.

Once the 5,000 meters got under way, the lead changed hands many times during the first third of the race. Guillemot knew of Nurmi's reputation, so he shadowed him throughout. It was his plan to follow Nurmi wherever and whenever he made a move.

Nurmi finally took over the lead at the 1,200 meter mark and Guillemot moved with him. Nurmi was capable of winning as a front runner or staying off the pace and then coming from behind to win. This day Nurmi's decision was to punish the field with a blistering front running race.

Nurmi was almost successful. Everyone but Guillemot fell by the wayside. Knowing that Guillemot was still shadowing him a few yards behind, Nurmi began his famous finishing kick when the bell rang for the last lap.

Astoundingly, Nurmi could not increase his lead and a few seconds later Guillemot began his own finishing kick. With 120 meters left in the race, Nurmi had lost his battle. Guillemot rushed past him and sprinted to the finish line, the winner by fifteen meters.

A few days later the two met again in the 10,000 meters. Though Guillemot passed Nurmi on the backstretch of the last lap to take the lead, the Finnish champion had learned his lesson from the 5,000 meters. Nurmi had kept something in reserve. With 75 meters left, he passed Guillemot and won by eight yards.

Nurmi will be remembered as the greatest distance runner ever, but Guillemot's claim to fame will be that he was, remarkably, one of the few men to ever defeat the legendary Finnish champion in the Olympic Games.

58

Edwin Moses

Los Angeles, 1984

The crowd of some 80,000 people was still buzzing with excitement at the Los Angeles Coliseum at 6:30 p.m. Sunday, August 5, 1984. Evelyn Ashford of the United States had just won the women's 100 meter final, creating an Olympic record. Now the athletes for the men's 400 meter hurdles final were stepping onto the track. The favorite in the race was 28-year-old Edwin Moses of the United States.

Eight years earlier at the 1976 Montreal Games, Moses won the gold medal by one of the greatest margins in the history of the event, defeating his teammate Michael Shine by more than a full second (about fifteen meters).

One year after the Montreal Games, Moses was defeated by Harald Schmid of West Germany. The loss had significance only in retrospect. Over the next seven years leading to the Los Angeles final, Moses would be undefeated — 102 successive victories including heats and finals. He was not able to compete in the 1980 Moscow Games because of the American boycott.

For Edwin Moses, the two years leading to the 1984 Los Angeles final had been filled with physical and emotional turmoil.

He could not compete in 1982 because of a series of injuries. When he returned his unbeaten streak was in jeopardy. But Moses began as he left off before the injury — never losing a race.

Several months before the Los Angeles Olympics, Edwin's beloved father, who had seen him win at the 1976 Games, died after a short illness.

"When I came onto the track for the final I found out that I was assigned lane number six, an outside lane," said Moses. "They had assigned the lanes the day before, but I didn't want to agonize over it the night before. Lane six gave me a bit of a disadvantage because the lanes were staggered, and being in one of the outside lanes I would not be able to see any of the run-

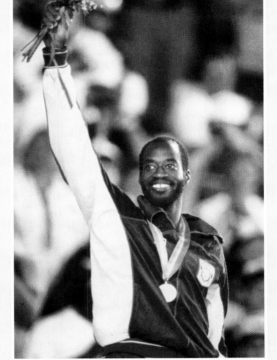

ners who would be a factor in the race because they were all to my left and behind me."

Sitting in one of the front row seats was Moses' wife, Myrella.

"There were so many things on his mind," said Myrella. "His unbeaten streak was still intact and before the race he told me and his mother that he was dedicating this race to his dad. And I was so helpless, because I couldn't do anything to help."

Moses' main opposition came from his teammate Danny Harris in lane four, and Harald Schmid, the last man to defeat him seven years earlier, in lane five. Hundreds of cameramen were clicking their cameras in anticipation of the start. Losing concentration, Moses and several others jumped the gun. None of the runners were charged with the false start.

"The noise was bothering me, for I needed full concentration to hear the starter," said Moses. "Actually, it gave me a few more moments for me to relax."

After 50 meters Moses took the lead. It was now apparent that without a major mishap, he was the class of the field.

"The hurdles approach you every 3½ to 4 seconds," said Moses. "I could feel I was moving away from the others. Things happen so quickly, there is not much time for thinking."

The crowd roared as Moses came off the final turn well in the lead, followed by Harris and Schmid. Once over the last hurdle down the stretch, the victory was his.

Moses, smiling, began his victory lap. Then he spotted his wife and mother, who had left their seats to join him on the field.

Edwin embraced them both and then began to cry.

"I won this one for dad. . . I won this one for dad," he said through his tears.

Mary Peters
Tokyo, 1964; Mexico City, 1968; Munich, 1972 Great Britain

Mary Peters of Great Britain still smiles today when people refer to her as an "overnight success." "If that's what they want to call seventeen years of competition, it's all right with me," says the beloved pentathlete.

Mary Peters began her Olympic career in the five-event pentathlon at the Tokyo 1964 Olympics, where she finished fourth. The pentathlon, five events considered a mini-decathlon, is contested over two days. The events test the women's ability to run, jump and throw. Points are earned for individual performance in each of the events, and the woman with the most total points at the end of the competition is the winner. Hypothetically, the gold medal can be won by a woman who has not won any of the individual tests but has been consistently high in all five events.

In her second Olympics in Mexico City, 29-year-old Mary Peters captained the women's team but her career appeared over when she finished ninth.

"When the 1972 Munich Games approached I knew this would be my last chance at winning a medal," said Peters. "I was 33 years old and time was running out."

The 100 meter hurdles was the first event and Peters finished second. In the shot-put, the second event, Mary got off a tremendous toss to win, and by doing so led the competition overall. The high jump was the final event of the first day and Peters was again superb. She won and increased her leading margin.

"I knew that I had to make the most of my first three events," recalled Peters, "because the long jump and 200 meters on the second day were not my best events."

In the first event of the second day Heide Rosendahl of West Germany, the world record holder in the long jump, had a tremendous victory, leaping almost three feet farther than Peters. Peters still led but Burglinde Pollack of East Germany, the pentathlon world record holder, and Rosendahl both were now within striking distance as they prepared for the 200 meters — the final event. Both Pollack and Rosendahl were expected to beat Peters, but if Mary could stay close enough at the finish, she would earn enough points to win the gold medal.

As expected, Rosendahl and Pollack finished ahead of Peters. Now there was a dramatic delay as the finishing times were converted into points. Finally the scoreboard flashed the news. Peters had won the gold medal, finishing ten points in front of Rosendahl and 33 points ahead of Pollack.

In her third Olympics and after seventeen years of competition "the old woman" had finally reached the top step of the victory podium and became "an overnight success."

Paavo Nurmi

Antwerp, 1920; Paris, 1924; Helsinki, 1952   Finland

At the approaches to the Helsinki Olympic stadium there is a bronze statue of Paavo Nurmi. It was dedicated in 1925 when 28-year-old Nurmi was still in his prime. It is rare that an athlete is so honored in his lifetime. Paavo Nurmi was that rare.

In the period immediately following World War I, Nurmi was the golden name in running in an era that is still known as the Golden Age of Sport. This era featured such legends as Jack Dempsey in boxing, Bobby Jones in golf, Bill Tilden in tennis and Red Grange in football. Nurmi was the only foreign-born athlete to make the list.

Nurmi began his Olympic career at the 1920 Antwerp Games. There he won the 10,000 meters and the silver in the 5,000 meters. He added two more gold in distance events no longer contested — the 8,000 meter individual cross country and the cross country team race.

Four years later in Paris Nurmi performed a feat that today still stands as the greatest individual track and field performance in history.

On July 10, 1924, Nurmi would attempt a "double" that seemed inconceivable. He was scheduled to run the 1,500 meters and a little more than one hour later the 5,000 meters. Never before had such an attempt been made.

Besides being fast and having unlimited endurance, Nurmi was a strategist. He calculated that if he reached various checkpoints at precisely exact times designed to punish the other runners, his physical condition and speed would be enough to carry him to victory.

During a race he was seen to be constantly glancing at his stopwatch. He would speed up or slow down to make certain that his pre-race strategy was met.

Nurmi won the 1,500 meters according to plan. Now in the 5,000 meters he would have to face his magnificent countryman Ville Ritola, who already had won two gold medals in distance events.

"With 300 meters left in the race I was in front of Paavo and feeling very strong," remembered Ritola. "Paavo tried to pass me but I held him off. For any other runner but Nurmi, that would have been the end of it. But on the final turn he made another surge. I could not believe that after running the 1,500 earlier, he still had the strength. But he did."

Nurmi added three more gold medals, two in team events and one in the individual cross country — all in races no longer on the Olympic program.

Four years later in Amsterdam, Nurmi won another gold in the 10,000 meters and two silver in the 5,000 meters and 3,000 meter steeplechase. He was now 31 years old.

Nurmi then made preparations to run the marathon at the 1932 Los Angeles Games, but he was not permitted to compete because of charges that he accepted money and was considered a professional.

Though not universally known, Nurmi was as successful a businessman as he was a runner, becoming one of Finland's wealthiest men through astute investments and as owner of a popular haberdashery shop. Yet, Nurmi was a contradiction — a man uncomfortable with his famous achievements. Because of his private nature, he appeared aloof — making it impossible for a once adoring public to embrace him.

At the 1952 Helsinki Games, 55-year-old Paavo Nurmi was given one final honor. Carrying the Olympic flame into the stadium as one of the final torchbearers, Nurmi was given a resounding ovation. As expressionless as he was during his career, paying little attention to the accolades accorded him, Nurmi left the arena without acknowledging the affection of the thousands who were honoring him.

On October 2, 1973, Paavo Nurmi died at age of 76. A state funeral was held at the famed Old Church of Helsinki.

Many of his former comrades from the Antwerp, Paris and Amsterdam Games still alive were there — athletes who because of Nurmi would be forever known as The Flying Finns.

Seventy-six-year-old Finnish President Urho Kekkonen, who was a high jumper and a teammate of Nurmi's on the 1924 national team, spoke the eulogy to his friend.

"When Nature removes a great man," said President Kekkonen, "people explore the horizons for a successor. But none comes and none will, for his class is extinguished with him."

Birger Ruud

Lake Placid, 1932; Garmisch-Partenkirchen, 1936; St. Moritz, 1948

Norway

It is very rare for an athlete to be more revered in defeat than in victory. Birger Ruud of Norway was one of those athletes.

At the 1932 Winter Olympic Games in Lake Placid, 20-year-old Birger Ruud entered his first Olympic event . . . the ski jump competition. Each contestant is given two jumps. The winner is determined by the total points earned in distance and style on each leap.

"The competition was difficult because there was very little snow," recalled Ruud. "They had to bring in snow by truck. We were able to go down the inrun without a problem, but the landing area was a combination of snow and dirt."

Nevertheless, after trailing in second place after the first round, Ruud got off a spectacular second leap and with excellent style points earned the gold medal.

Two years later Ruud won the famed Holmenkollen ski jump — the legendary hill in Oslo used but once a year for the internationally famous event. Already a national hero because of his Olympic win, Ruud now became a legend when he won the Holmenkollen.

"To win an Olympic gold medal is glorious; to win the Holmenkollen is ecstasy," recalled Ruud. "Now I had won them both."

Two years later at the 1936 Winter Games in Garmisch-Partenkirchen, Germany, Ruud again entered the 90 meter ski jump competition in an attempt to make Olympic history — to become the first man in history to win successive ski jumping gold medals.

With Chancellor Adolf Hitler in attendance, Ruud was again superb. He won his second gold medal.

"I looked forward to winning again in 1940," recalled Birger sadly. "But it was not to be. The 1940 and 1944 Games were canceled because of World War II. I was put in jail for two years by the Nazis, who occupied our country. They tried to get Norwegian athletes to support their cause, but I would have none of it. So they put me in jail."

When the Winter Games were renewed in St. Moritz in 1948, Birger Ruud was 36 years old and an assistant coach on the Norwegian ski jumping team. The night

before the competition was to begin the weather turned ugly, and the Norwegians believed the conditions might be too dangerous for one of their younger jumpers. It was decided that Birger Ruud would replace him. In one of the most amazing comebacks in Olympic history, Ruud won the silver medal — twelve years after he won his last gold.

All three ski jumping medals were won by Norwegians, but the loudest cheers at the victory platform ceremony honoring the winners were for the man who won the silver — the immortal Birger Ruud.

Silken Laumann

Barcelona, 1992

Canada 🍁

In the summer of 1991 it was predicted that Silken Laumann of Canada would be the favorite to win the women's single sculls at the Barcelona Olympics one year later.

She had just completed a remarkable season. Silken Laumann was the overall winner in a series of six races for the World Cup and then in a single race in Vienna was crowned world champion. Honor after honor was bestowed upon her, including being named the Canadian athlete of the year.

In May 1992, with a little more than two months before the Barcelona Olympics, Silken Laumann was competing in a pre-Olympic race in Essen, Germany. Before the race, tragedy struck.

"I was just starting to warm up when out of nowhere was this German boat," remembered Laumann. "It crashed right into my right leg, severing all the muscles, tendons and ligaments from midway up my right shin all the way down to my ankle."

The injury was so severe, the initial medical report was that she would never row again. A little later, the news was less ominous. It was determined that with rest and rehabilitation she would get back into competition but certainly not in time for the Barcelona Olympics, just two months away. One of the lone dissenters was Silken Laumann.

"The first goal I set for myself was the Barcelona Olympics," remembered Laumann. "I didn't know if it was possible. When I looked at the big open wound, I sort of wondered whether it was possible."

Rehabilitation and training were frustrating and painful, both physically and mentally.

"There were many tears," said her coach, Mike Spracklen, "because Silken is an emotional person. But it was not the sort of sadness that, 'I'm not going to make it,' but rather, 'When am I going to make it?' She wanted

to go to the Olympics, and no one was going to stop her from going."

Five weeks after the accident and one month before the Barcelona Games, Silken Laumann made the dramatic announcement that she was going to Barcelona. Her priorities had changed. Immediately after the injury, her goal was to compete. Now she was going after one of the medals.

Incredibly, on August 2, 1992, Silken Laumann was one of the six finalists in the 2,000 meter single sculls at the Barcelona Games.

Throughout most of the race, Silken Laumann trailed in fourth place behind Elisabeta Lipa of Romania, Annelies Bredael of Belgium and Anne Marden of the United States.

"With about 1,000 meters to go I thought I was going to die. I knew I couldn't win but I wanted one of the medals," said Laumann. "I said to myself, 'I'm not coming in fourth.' Fourth is the worst position — to just miss a medal."

Silken Laumann set her sights on America's Anne Marden in third place. Inch by inch she moved closer to the American. Finally, a few meters before the finish, she was in third place, trailing behind Lipa of Romania and Bredael of Belgium, second.

At the victory platform ceremony for the three medal winners, one columnist was already writing the lead paragraph to his story. The words:

"Canada won four gold medals and one bronze in rowing at the Barcelona Olympics. Let the word go out that on this occasion Silken Laumann's bronze medal shines as brightly in the Barcelona sun as any of the gold."

Despite torn muscles, tendons and ligaments from her shin to her ankle, Canada's Silken Laumann went on to claim the bronze medal in the women's single sculls.

Spiridon Louis

Historically and emotionally, Athens, Greece, was the only city that could be considered to host the first revival of the modern Olympic Games in 1896. From a practical financial standpoint, no choice could have been worse.

Greece was beset with financial problems. The government would have much difficulty financing the Games. Only a gift from a Greek millionaire philanthropist made it possible for a new marble stadium to be constructed.

The first Olympics were a "catch as catch can" affair. There were no national Olympic committees, no formal teams. A total of fourteen countries and 245 athletes, many paying their own way, entered. With national pride at stake, Greece provided the most athletes. The thousands of spectators, mostly Greek, anticipated their countrymen would do well in the track and field events since their heroes from the ancient Greek Games had been immortalized by poets, artists and sculptors.

When the competition got under way, disaster after disaster followed the Greek athletes. American athletes won nine of the eleven track and field events. Australia won the other two. The Greek athletes could not win a single event and thousands of fans came alive with derisive muttering — an 1896 version of "Yankee Go Home."

On the final day of the track and field competition, with some Greek newspapermen blasting the professionalism of the Americans

and calling for the end to this "athletic farce," the marathon run was scheduled.

Losing this historic race would be the final "stab in the heart" for Greece, since the history of the marathon is etched in its culture and tradition. Every Greek schoolchild is taught the epic story of the Battle of Marathon in 490 B.C., when 7,000 Greek warriors defeated 20,000 invading Persians on the Plains of Marathon, a sea town some 40 kilometers from Athens.

Historians would later call the great Greek victory "the battle that saved Western civilization as we know it today." After the battle, a lone runner was sent from Marathon to Athens to tell the populace of the great triumph. When he reached the Athens center, he exhaustedly called out, "Nenikikamen" ("We are Victorious"). Then he collapsed and died.

Now more than 2,000 years later, the marathon would start at the site of the historic battle. The starter's gun sent the seventeen contestants off. At various times throughout the race runners from France and Australia led. The progress of the race was sent ahead to the stadium by messengers on horseback and bicycle. The spectators were depressed.

But as the first of the runners approached the stadium, an excited horseman entered the stadium at full gallop and made his way to the Royal Box, where Prince George and Prince Constantine, sons of King George, were seated. The 70,000 people watched for a sign. An excited whisper became a roar. Finally it was confirmed. A Greek runner was in the lead.

Minutes went by and then it happened. Into the stadium came the Greek runner, a shepherd named Spiridon

AMERICAN AND GREEK VICTORS, CONTESTANTS AND OFFICIALS OF THE OLYMPIC GAMES.

Louis. He was exhausted but slowly made his way down the straightaway toward the finish line. The crowd exploded, and the emotional outburst urged the shepherd on.

Prince George and Prince Constantine leaped from their box to the track and formed an honor guard on either side of Louis. The three ran together to the finish line. The thousands of spectators watching hugged and kissed, some crying hysterically. The pride of Greece had been restored.

Following the victory, the press and public rejoiced in the magnificence of the first Olympiad and that plans should be made for its continuance. The Olympic Games had passed its first hurdle and a Greek shepherd, Spiridon Louis, was mostly responsible for it. For as Louis crossed the finish line, many of the weeping spectators were whispering those historic words, "Nenikikamen, We are Victorious."

Andrea Mead Lawrence

United States

Of all the amazing performances in Olympic alpine skiing, nothing could compare to the one that took place in the women's slalom event at the 1952 Oslo Olympics. It was there that Andrea Mead Lawrence of the United States performed a feat that will never be duplicated.

Andrea Mead Lawrence was already a gold medal winner at the Oslo Games when she stood at the top of the hill awaiting her turn in the women's slalom — an event that consists of two runs down a course of 38 gates.

Earlier in the week she amazed the skiing world by winning the giant slalom by more than two seconds over her nearest competitor. In an event that is usually won by infinitesimal parts of a second, her overwhelming victory had many experts believing the timing watches had malfunctioned.

A few days later Lawrence started down the course in the downhill event. At the various checkpoints she was far in the lead, but inexplicably she fell and was out of contention.

With one event left, the slalom, Lawrence still had a good chance of winning her second gold medal. Lawrence was the fifth skier scheduled to go down the course. The winner is decided by the combined lowest time of the two runs.

On the upper part of the hill, as in the giant slalom and downhill, Lawrence was the fastest of all. But in the middle of the course her ski caught a gate and before she could stop herself she had gone ten meters past the gate. Fortunately she kept her balance and did not fall.

After quickly backtracking to the gate, Lawrence continued down the course. Amazingly, when the first round was over Lawrence was in fourth place, 1.2 seconds behind the first round leader.

Most experts would have counted her out, for the time she would have to make up was considerable. But there was not a spectator there who didn't remember her victory earlier in the giant slalom.

On her second run Lawrence was spectacular, fast and flawless. When the final skier finished the run, Andrea Mead Lawrence was in front by eight-tenths of a second over the second place finisher. It was estimated that if she had not clipped the gate in her first run, Lawrence would have won by at least five seconds.

Andrea Mead Lawrence had done the impossible, and with it she became the first American ever to win two alpine skiing gold medals.

Lasse Viren

Munich, 1972; Montreal, 1976    Finland

The massacre of the Israeli athletes in the Olympic Village and the seven swimming gold medals won by Mark Spitz at the 1972 Munich Games all but overshadowed one of the great running performances in Olympic history, turned in by 23-year-old Lasse Viren of Finland.

In the preliminary heat of the 10,000 meters Viren's fourth place finish gave him a qualifying position for the finals.

Three days later the final of the 10,000 meters was held. Most experts predicted that the battle for the gold medal would be between Dave Bedford of Great Britain and Emiel Puttemans of Belgium. Each had broken the Olympic record in his qualifying heat.

With the race less than half over, Bedford was in the lead. A few yards back Puttemans was in fourth place, followed by Viren. Suddenly, without warning, Viren tripped and fell, taking another of the pre-race favorites, Mohamed Gammoudi of Tunisia, down with him.

"I still do not know what caused the accident," said Viren afterward. "My only thought was to get up as quickly as possible. I was very fortunate that I was not trampled by the others."

Viren lost more than 50 meters because of his fall. However, with still half the race left, he was able to make contact with the front runners quickly. Gammoudi was not so fortunate. After one more lap he had to retire from the race. Viren, amazingly, was as strong as ever. He took over the lead and held off the last lap charge of Puttemans to win the gold medal.

With this one heroic victory, Lasse Viren brought back the glory of Finland's past. The country that brought to the Olympic arena the legendary Paavo Nurmi and his band of Flying Finns, who dominated the long distance events in the 1920s and through the 1936 Berlin Games, had been reborn. Viren had given them their first gold medal in 36 years.

A few days later Viren stepped to the starting line for the 5,000 meters against many of the great internationalists he defeated in the 10,000.

Once again Viren was superb. He not only broke the Olympic record but joined his countryman Hannes Kolehmainen, Emil Zatopek of Czechoslovakia and the Soviet Union's Vladimir Kuts as the only men to win both the 5,000 and 10,000 meters in the same Olympics.

Injuries plagued Viren leading to the 1976 Montreal Games. Several ligaments that had caused him constant pain in his leg had to be removed.

Because he had not had many victories between Munich and Montreal, Viren was still an unknown factor. Nevertheless, he entered the 10,000 and 5,000 meters.

After his 10,000 meter victory in 1972 stories circulated throughout Munich that Viren was a "blood booster," a controversial practice in which the athlete has blood extracted from his body, then has it reinserted before a competition. Purportedly "blood boosting" increases the body's oxygen intake, thus providing greater endurance capabilities.

After denying these claims, Viren added new mystery to his performances suggesting that he trained on a diet of reindeer milk.

With one lap to go in the 1976 Montreal 10,000, Viren, in second place, started his patented finishing kick that skyrocketed him to victory.

Then a few days later, incredibly, Viren held off several challenges over the last two laps in the 5,000 meters to give him his fourth successive Olympic gold medal. Lasse Viren had done what no one else had ever done — win the 5,000 and 10,000 meter events at two successive Olympics.

The day after his 5,000 the world was amazed to see Lasse Viren at the starting line for the marathon — the grueling, 26 mile 385 yard last event on the Olympic program. In his first marathon ever, Viren finished fifth.

Sammy Lee

London, 1948; Helsinki, 1952

United States

World War II was over, but three years later many of the athletes at the 1948 London Olympics were still in military uniform. One of them was 28-year-old diver Lt. Sammy Lee, an American Korean who was unable to compete in his prime at the 1940 and 1944 Olympics, which were canceled during World War II. Now as an Army doctor specializing in ear, nose and throat, Sammy was determined to make up for much of the frustration that followed him after the Japanese attack on Pearl Harbor on December 7, 1941.

"In the early days of the war, my Asian looks made my life miserable," remembered Sammy. "When I went to public pools to practice, I used to hear people whispering, "What's that little Jap doing here?" and, "Does the FBI know whether he's a spy?"

Once in the Army, Sammy's reputation was secure, but when the war ended he still believed he had a message to send. "Nobody knew anything about Korea," Sammy remembered solemnly, "since we were for so many years controlled by the Japanese. I wanted to show the world what a Korean could do if he had the opportunity."

In the London Olympic platform diving event Sammy Lee was in first place with one dive left. "I remember the last dive in London — a forward three and a half somersault which I invented. When I hit the water I thought I hit 'flat'. . . you tingle all over till the pain starts in your stomach," Sammy recalled. "I was afraid to look at the judges because I thought I would get zeros. Then I saw lots of 'tens' and 'nine and a halfs.' The gold medal was mine. This was pretty good for a guy who never learned how to swim."

Sammy Lee retired and continued his medical career, but as the 1952 Helsinki Olympic Games approached, he contracted a well-known athletic disease called "Olympic fever," the desire to keep on competing.

Now 32, Major Sammy Lee was competing against much younger divers. But again he was impeccable, becoming the first diver in Olympic history to win two successive platform gold medals.

"You can't look back," smiles Sammy. "But if it weren't

for the war I would be alone in the record book with four platform diving gold medals."

Sammy's Olympic contributions continued after he retired from active competition. His protégé Bob Webster won the platform gold medal at the 1960 Rome Olympics and came back four years later to win in Tokyo — at the time, the only other man to win successive platform diving gold medals.

Still later Sammy became the first coach of a young diver whom he spotted at a local pool and soon recognized that under his tutelage could become one of the greatest divers ever. The boy's name was Greg Louganis, who later went on to win the "double-double" (successive springboard and platform diving gold medals) at the 1984 Los Angeles and 1988 Seoul Olympic Games.

Nadia Comaneci

At the European gymnastic championships in 1975, one year before the Montreal Olympics, thirteen-year-old Nadia Comaneci of Romania skyrocketed to international prominence by winning four of the five events contested.

Team gymnastics for women had been on the Olympic program since the 1928 Amsterdam Games, but individual competition did not begin until the 1952 Helsinki Olympics, coinciding with the Soviet Union's first participation in the Games. In Helsinki and the Olympics that followed, Soviet women gymnasts moved to the forefront of international competitions.

As the 1976 Montreal Olympics approached, however, their female superstars would face a formidable opponent — fourteen-year-old Nadia Comaneci of Romania.

In the team competition the Soviet women, as expected, won the title. But it was Nadia Comaneci who captivated the thousands in the arena and the millions of TV viewers throughout the world.

In the uneven bar segment of the team competition Comaneci performed brilliantly, and the crowd, now silent, anticipated a historic moment as they waited for her score to be flashed.

There was a roar of surprise as the number "one" flashed on the scoreboard. It was soon realized that Comaneci had upset modern technology. The scoring sys-

tem had not been programmed to register a "ten," which is perfection. Finally the public address announcer cleared up the confusion, announcing that Nadia had indeed been awarded a perfect "ten" by the judges.

"I knew my routine was flawless," said Nadia afterward. "I had performed it many times before in practice the same way."

Though Romania finished second behind the Soviet Union in the team competition after the optional segments one day later, it was Nadia who held the imagination of the spectators and her fellow gymnasts. She received her second and third perfect "tens" in the uneven bars and the balance beam.

Two days later, she humbled the great Soviet champions in the individual all-around, the rising star, Nelli Kim, and the 1972 all-around champion, Lyudmila Turishcheva. In winning, Nadia again was given perfect tens in the uneven bars and balance beam.

The following day, with five "tens" already hers, she picked up two more in the individual balance beam and uneven bar competitions.

When the week was over, Nadia had been awarded seven "tens" in winning three gold, one silver and one bronze medal. Almost forgotten was the fact that she became the first Romanian in history to win an Olympic gymnastic gold medal.

Jean-Claude Killy 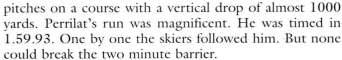 Grenoble, 1968   France

France's Jean-Claude Killy is considered by many the greatest all around alpine skier in history, but it was not apparent at the 1964 Innsbruck Games. There Killy competed in all three alpine events, the downhill, slalom and giant slalom. He came away with no medals, his best effort, a fifth place finish in the giant slalom.

Between Innsbruck and the 1968 Grenoble Games, Killy's career skyrocketed. He became a favorite to medal in all three events. The downhill was scheduled first. "Just one month before the Grenoble Olympics, I couldn't win a race," Killy recalls. "The year before I won nine out of ten downhills, but now I was uncertain. I had many doubts whether I could put it all together."

His countryman, Guy Perillat, was the first starter in the downhill, the most dangerous and thrilling alpine event. The skier faced a series of bumps, ruts and deep

pitches on a course with a vertical drop of almost 1000 yards. Perrilat's run was magnificent. He was timed in 1.59.93. One by one the skiers followed him. But none could break the two minute barrier.

The 14th skier was Jean-Claude Killy. He would have to go all out to defeat his countryman since the downhill consisted of only one run. Unlike the slalom races there was no way to make up for a poor run in the downhill. When Killy finished the crowd roared its acclaim. The scoreboard flashed the time.

He beat Perrilat by eight hundredths of a second. Killy and Perrilat were the only two skiers to break the two minute mark, and France won the gold and silver medals.

Killy's next event was the giant slalom. "I had a lot of confidence in this one," recalls Killy. "The race is decided by the lowest total time of two runs — competed on successive days." Killy led after the first day and increased his lead on the second run. He won by more than two seconds for his second gold medal.

Finally it was time for the slalom, another two run event. The final outcome is still cause for major discussion today. With visibility almost at zero, the race in the fog was a farce. Killy was in first place after his two runs, but Austria's Karl Schranz had a chance to beat him with a fast second run. It appeared that Schranz was about to defeat Killy when suddenly down the course the Austrian braked. A mysterious figure had appeared in his path. Schranz protested and was given a second run.

This time Schranz finished without incident. His time was better than Killy's total. For two hours he thought he was the winner, but a review board came to the conclusion that Schranz had missed two gates on the 'mysterious stranger' first run and never should have been given a second run. He was disqualified and Killy was named the winner.

Killy had duplicated Austria's feat of Tony Sailer twelve years before in Cortina d'Ampezzo.

55

79

Harrison Dillard

When Jesse Owens returned to his home in Cleveland, Ohio, after winning four gold medals at the 1936 Berlin Olympic Games, he was given a ticker tape parade. One of the thousands who turned out to greet Jesse was 13-year-old Harrison Dillard.

"I remember running back home and bursting into the kitchen, yelling, 'Mama, Mama. I just saw Jesse Owens and I'm going to be just like him'," laughed Dillard more than a half century later.

"My mother just smiled and said, 'Yes, son, I'm sure you will'."

Dillard never got to run in the Olympics until the 1948 London Games. He probably would have won a couple of gold medals in 1944 if the Games were not cancelled because of World War II.

Dillard first gained fame when he was still in the Army and competed in the GI Olympics after Germany was defeated in the summer of 1945. Dillard won four gold medals and General George S. Patton greeted him with the words, "You're the best damn athlete I've ever seen." This was no small compliment, for Patton was a teammate of the legendary Jim Thorpe when both competed at the 1912 Stockholm Games.

Leading to the 1948 London Games, Dillard had a winning streak of 82 consecutive victories, mostly in the hurdles. At the Olympic Trials Dillard faltered in his specialty. The man who was predicted to be a certain gold medal winner hit several hurdles and incredibly failed to finish the race.

But fortunately, the day before, as a tuneup for the hurdles, he finished third in the 100 meters and qualified for both the 100 meters and the 4 x 100 relay.

Given little chance in London, Dillard amazed the athletic world by winning the 100 meters in a photo finish victory over his teammate, Barney Ewell. Later, he ran the third leg on the victorious United States 4 x 100 relay team.

Dillard continued to compete and four years later at age 28 he finally qualified for the Olympics in his favorite event, the 110 meter hurdles.

This time at the 1952 Helsinki Olympics Dillard was determined. In the 110 meter hurdles final, he was impeccable going over the hurdles and defeated his teammate, Jack Davis, in a photo finish.

A few days later he ran the second leg on another United States 4 x 100 victorious relay team for his fourth gold medal.

"When I mounted the victory stand for the fourth time," remembered Dillard, "I was so proud. All I could think of was that time I ran running home to my mother after the Jesse Owens victory parade and saying to her, 'I'm going to be just like him'."

As seen by the photo-finish camera, Harrison Dillard edges out countryman Barney Ewell (second) and L. Labeach (Panama, third) in the final of the 100 meters.

Greg Louganis
Los Angeles, 1984; Seoul 1988 United States

The crowd at the 1976 Montreal Olympic platform diving competition groaned as sixteen-year-old Greg Louganis of the United States botched his ninth and next-to-last dive. This lone mishap paved the way for 28-year-old Klaus Dibiasi of Italy to win his third successive platform diving title, the only diver in Olympic history to perform such a feat.

After the awards ceremony Dibiasi announced his retirement. "Now I can sit back and watch you win in Moscow," said Dibiasi as he embraced Louganis.

Of course, Dibiasi was wrong. When the United States boycotted the 1980 Moscow Olympics, Louganis, an overwhelming choice to win both the springboard and diving gold medals, was forced to watch the diluted diving competition on television.

At the 1984 Los Angeles Games, 24-year-old Louganis was superb. After winning the springboard event by the largest amount of points in Olympic history, he now stood poised for his tenth and final dive in the platform event , ready to make history again — to become the first diver ever to score more than 700 points.

His final dive was a reverse 3½ somersault in the tuck position. Not only does this dive have the highest degree of difficulty, but it bears the ominous name — "the Dive of Death." One year earlier Louganis was competing at the World University Games in Edmonton, Canada, and witnessed a Soviet diver attempting the same dive. "I had a premonition," Louganis recalled. "I knew something terrible had happened when I felt the tower shake. I heard screaming and ran to the pool's edge and saw blood in the water.

The Soviet diver had hit his head on the platform and was unconscious in the water. One week later he died."

Now in Los Angeles, Louganis prepared for the same dive. He paused longer than usual. Then he leaped off the tower. He emerged from the water hearing tremendous applause. The spectators and judges agreed. One judge gave him a perfect 10 and the rest gave him 9's and 9.5's. His final score was more than 10 points better than the magical 700 mark.

Four years later in Seoul, Louganis made the attempt for the "double-double"— successive victories in both the springboard and diving events.

In the preliminary round of the springboard, disaster struck. On his ninth dive his head struck the board and, in total disarray, he crashed into the water. Fortunately his injury was not serious. He went on to qualify, setting the stage for his victory in the springboard the next day.

Later Louganis found himself in a head-to-head duel with a fourteen-year-old Chinese diver in the platform final. With one dive left, Xiong Ni of China led Greg by three points. Ni's last dive was near perfect. Louganis had to be impeccable to win. Incredibly, his last dive was the reverse 3½ somersault in the tuck position. . . "the Dive of Death."

Without hesitation Louganis walked to the platform edge and dove. The crowd roared. The dive was spectacular. Greg Louganis had completed the "double-double" and joined America's woman champion, Pat McCormick (1952–1956) as the only two divers ever to accomplish this feat.

83

Vera Cáslavská

Mexico City, 1968   Czechoslovakia

Perhaps the two most significant political demonstrations surrounding an international athletic event took place at the 1968 Mexico City Olympic Games.

The most famous was the "Black Power salute" performed on the award podium by America's Tommie Smith and John Carlos, the first and third place finishers in the 200 meters. . . a protest against the inferior treatment given United States blacks.

Another dramatic moment took place in the gymnastic competition involving Vera Cáslavská of Czechoslovakia, the undisputed Queen of the Games.

Four years earlier in Tokyo, Cáslavská thrilled the gymnastic world by dethroning the Soviet Union's legendary Larissa Latynina for the individual all-around title. Latynina still holds the Olympic record for the most medals won, with eighteen. . . nine gold, five silver and four bronze.

Now, four years later, Cáslavská, at age 26, arrived in Mexico City just two months after Soviet Union troops had moved into Czechoslovakia to quell free speech. Cáslavská was as spectacular in Mexico City as she was in Tokyo, not only retaining her all-around title but adding a medal in every gymnastic event — four gold and two silver.

But the most poignant moment for Cáslavská took place during the victory ceremony at the conclusion of the floor exercise event. Vera had to share the gold medal with Larissa Petrik of the Soviet Union. Protocol called for the playing of each of the national anthems in honor of Czechoslovakia and the Soviet Union.

A smiling Cáslavská stood tall and straight as the Czech national anthem was played first.

Immediately after, the Soviet Union anthem was played. The smile left Cáslavská's face and she bowed her head. There was no mistaking her emotions or the political implications.

One day later there was joy again in the life of Vera Cáslavská. She was married to Josef Odlozil, who competed earlier in the 1,500 meters on the track. More than 10,000 fans waited outside the church. When she appeared, the crowd roared their acclaim which confirmed that she was one of the most beloved athletes to appear at the Mexico City Games.

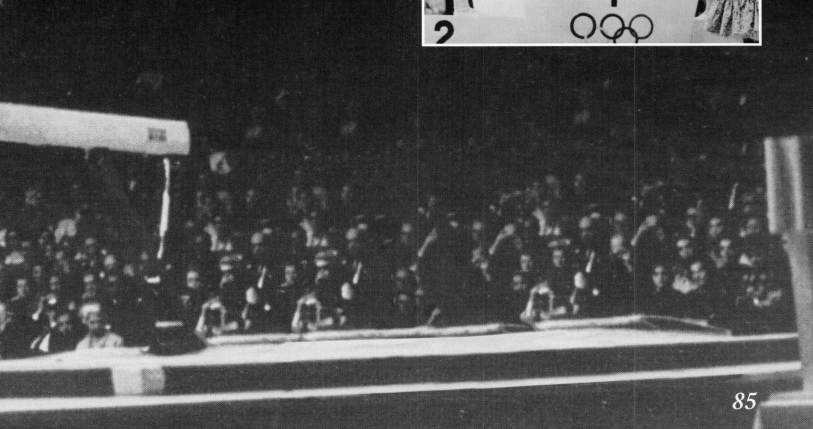

Michael Gross

Los Angeles, 1984   West Germany

At 4:15 p.m. on the afternoon of July 29, 1984, 20-year-old Michael Gross of West Germany, the world record holder, waited for the start of the 200 meter freestyle final. The six-foot, seven-inch Gross was nicknamed "The Albatross" because his arms extended in a wing span of more than seven feet, propelling him through the water faster than any swimmer in the world. Within the next 26 hours, Gross would be attempting a Herculean task — swimming in the 200 meter freestyle, and the 100 meter butterfly and anchoring the West German 4 x 200 freestyle relay.

When the gun sent the swimmers off, most predicted that Gross' main opponent would be his own 200 meter freestyle world record rather than the other finalists.

Gross took the lead immediately and increased it with every stroke. When he touched the wall at the finish, he was more than a body length in front of America's Michael Heath. There were two additional honors for Gross. He broke his own world record and became the first West German ever to win an Olympic gold medal in swimming.

Twenty-four hours later Gross was back for the 100 meter butterfly, but he was not the favorite. Top honors were expected to go to Pablo Morales of the United States, who set the world record in the Olympic trials and earlier that day in his qualifications set an Olympic record, less than a half second off his own world record. Morales and Gross were the only finalists to swim the distance under 54 seconds.

Morales got off quickly and at the halfway point touched the wall a few inches in front of Gross.

Morales maintained his slight lead as they moved down the last 50 meters, but with each stroke, Gross was inching closer. Finally, with ten meters left, Gross overtook Morales and touched the wall to set a world record, his second within 24 hours. Remarkably, Morales, fifteen-hundredths of a second behind, also bettered his own former mark.

"Pablo was very upset," said Gross. "He has swum the fastest race of his life, only to lose. I told him that he

should not be unhappy, because he had done his best. He said, 'Thank you,' but he was very unhappy."

One hour and fifteen minutes later the 4 x 200 meter relay was scheduled. Michael Gross was assigned to swim the anchor leg for the West German team.

Gross' greatness caused a shift in strategy for the American team, which in the preliminary round broke the West German world record. USA Coach Don Gambrill decided to put his quickest swimmers in the first three positions to give Bruce Hayes, their unheralded anchor man known for his fast finishes, a lead that Gross could not overtake.

The American strategy backfired. When Hayes started off for his anchor leg, his lead was only a second and a half over Gross.

"Gross' best time is two and a half seconds better than mine," said Hayes. "So I was hoping for a three or four second lead. But that didn't happen."

Gross immediately went after Hayes and halfway through their 200 meter leg the Albatross had drawn even. They were both swimming at a pace that would smash the world record. As they approached 150 meters, Gross took the lead.

"The dreams I had were coming true," said Hayes. "Before this race I would have terrible dreams that these long arms would be catching me and now it was happening."

"I was getting tired. It was my third big race," said Gross. "I was hoping to go farther ahead and lose contact with him."

In the last 50 meters, Gross' tiredness was becoming evident. Hayes was inching up to him again and the predominantly American crowd was cheering him on.

Incredibly, Hayes forged ahead of Gross and touched the wall first. The Americans had broken the world record by more than three seconds. In defeat Gross had swum the fastest 200 meter relay leg ever.

As the swimmers left the pool, a tremendous ovation began for Michael Gross. . . who in victory and defeat gained Olympic glory. And those who faced Michael Gross will forever remember the experience — the better for their meeting with The Albatross.

"At a given place on a given day at a given time — something magical can happen," is a belief that is shared by every athlete during the Parade of Nations at the Opening Ceremonies of the Olympic Games. For most of the thousands of athletes who have competed through the decades that moment of "magic" remains an unfulfilled dream. But there was one obscure athlete who reached for the stars at the 1964 Tokyo Olympics — and miraculously, was able to grab hold.

Billy Mills, an American Indian, wasn't even the best United States 10,000 meter runner entered in Tokyo. He finished a distant second to his teammate Gerry Lindgren in the Olympic trials. Lindgren thus became America's hope to perhaps win one of the medals against a super star-studded field of international runners.

The unanimous favorite was Ron Clarke of Australia, the world record holder. Also given good chances at the gold medal were Pyotr Bolotnikov, who won the event four years earlier in Rome, and New Zealand's Murray Halberg, who won the 5,000 meters at the same Games. But they would have strong opposition from Mohamed Gammoudi of Tunisia and Mamo Wolde of Ethiopia. Practically every expert predicted that Mills would do well to finish in the first ten.

"My strategy was simply to go out with the top four runners and stay in contact and hope for the best," recalled Mills. "But when we reached the halfway mark, I was within one second of my fastest 5,000 meters ever and *there was still 5,000 meters to go*. I said to myself, 'I'm going to have to quit.'"

Rather than quit, Mills started to sprint, and he took the lead. "I knew where my wife, Patricia, was sitting in the stands and I happened to glance up at the spot where she was, so if I quit, maybe she wouldn't see me. My thoughts were that she was crying and not so much the fact that she knew I was ready to quit. Together we had made a commitment . . . we had a goal and I was pursuing it, and there was really no way that I could quit."

As they began the last lap, the lead runners not only had to worry about each other but had to find their way around several "lapped" runners.

In the melee Clarke, trying to pass Mills, bumped him back to third. Gammoudi took advantage of Mills' stumble and moved past Clarke and Mills and the race appeared over.

"Something inside me was saying, 'There's still a chance, there's still a chance,'" recalled Mills. "So I started driving. They were fifteen yards in front of me, but it seemed like 50 yards," said Mills. "Then I kept telling myself, 'I can win. . . I can win. . . I can win. . .' and the next thing I remember I broke the tape."

The crowd was hysterical.

"A Japanese official came running up to me and he put his hands on my shoulders and with a strange look said, 'Who are you?'" laughed Mills. "And then I thought, 'Oh my God. . . I miscounted the laps.' Then he smiled and said, 'You finished. . . you finished. . .' and I knew I had won."

Billy Mills had created perhaps the greatest upset in Olympic track and field history and with it became the only American to ever win the 10,000 meter event.

1956 Water Polo

Melbourne, 1956   Hungary/USSR

Olympic tradition dating back to ancient Greece calls for the cessation of fighting between warring nations during the Olympic Games. This was to insure safe passage for the athletes traveling to and from the Games.

Sadly this tradition was violated in modern times when the Games took an eight-year hiatus because of World War I (1912–1920) and later a twelve-year stoppage due to World War II (1936–1948).

In the post–World War II era, international strife caused many nations to defect from competing in various Olympics — in particular the United States boycott of the 1980 Moscow Games and the subsequent retaliation by the Soviet Union four years later in Los Angeles.

As the 1956 Melbourne Games approached, two major "hot spots" threatened the Games. Great Britain and France occupied the Suez Canal after an Israeli attack on Egypt and so Egypt, Lebanon and Iraq refused to send teams.

Equally explosive was the Soviet Union incursion into Hungary, resulting in much death and destruction. In protest, some countries also did not compete. Ironically, both Hungary and the Soviet Union sent teams but support for the Hungarians was almost unanimous.

Once the Games got under way, each day the world awaited the possible athletic confrontation between the athletes of Hungary and the Soviet Union.

After many minor incidents, mostly verbal abuse directed at the Soviets, the two nations met in the water polo competition. The meeting between the two teams was as one-sided as the military confrontation. Hungary for years had the best water polo team in the world and the Soviets were not in their league. Thousands of pro-Hungarian spectators jammed the arena to support their countrymen.

The game was a vicious one, with much abuse taking place underwater, out of sight of the judges. The crowd roared throughout the game as the Hungarians built up a 4 to nothing lead with just a few minutes to play.

Then, before a hysterically happy audience sensing victory, a Hungarian player emerged from a melee beneath the water with a slashing wound beneath his eye administered by a frustrated Soviet opponent. Hisses and boos pervaded the hall and hundreds of Hungarians moved from their seats to poolside, ready to attack the team that to them represented the horror that had befallen their country.

Police were called in to repress the angry spectators and a conference of officials took place. With much wisdom the officials decided the game was over and declared Hungary the winner. There was no protest from the Soviets.

The competition went on without further incident. But the pent-up anger of the Hungarians had spilled over into great athletic achievement. The Hungarians went on to an undefeated record in water polo — seven victories and no defeats to win the gold medal. The Soviet Union finished third.

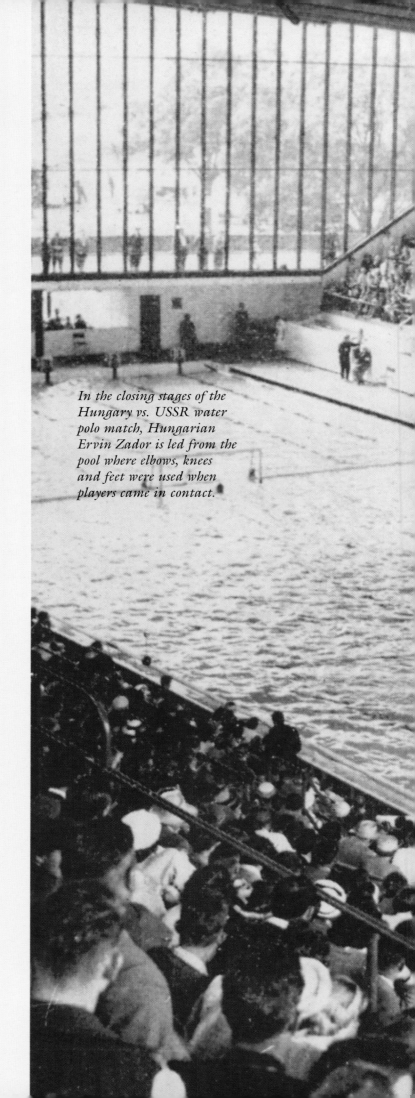

In the closing stages of the Hungary vs. USSR water polo match, Hungarian Ervin Zador is led from the pool where elbows, knees and feet were used when players came in contact.

Olga Korbut

Munich, 1972   USSR

Probably the most poignant scene emanating from the gymnastic competition at the 1972 Munich Olympics was when television cameras honed in on seventeen-year-old Olga Korbut of the Soviet Union weeping bitterly after botching her performance on the uneven bars in her bid for top honors in the women's all-around competition.

The young Soviet gymnast had two days earlier captivated worldwide audiences with her skill and innovative moves as part of the gold medal winning Soviet team, climaxing her scintillating performance with a captivating smile that endeared her to millions. Television audiences shared in her despair as Korbut's mishaps totally eliminated her from competing for top honors.

The scenes of Olga weeping were played and replayed on television and in disaster she gained more affection throughout the world than her teammate Lyudmila Turishcheva, who won the all-around gold medal.

24 hours later Korbut made one of the great comebacks in the history of the Olympics when she competed in the individual apparatus events. Now with the disaster of the uneven bar mishap behind her, Olga, smiling brilliantly, won two gold and a silver and changed the face of gymnastics forever — particularly the image usually associated with the dour, unemotional appearance of the Soviet athlete.

Olga's personality was not looked upon favorably in the Soviet Union. There her individuality was frowned upon, and she was criticized unmercifully by the press and fellow athletes for becoming a "Western cult star" and exploiting her worldwide acclaim at the expense of the team.

In the United States she became a matinee idol and changed the sport from virtual obscurity to one that became available to thousands of potential new "Olgas." One United States official said, "Before Olga came on to the scene there were less than 15,000 American female gymnasts. Two years after the Munich Games there were 50,000, and we receive almost a hundred letters a week from young girls wanting to know how they can become another Olga."

Korbut was voted the Female Athlete of the Year in 1972 by the Associated Press and numerous international press agencies, but with all the accolades that have been showered upon her, there is one she finds the most special.

"In 1973 after the Munich Games I was brought to the White House to meet President Nixon," she said with her broad smile. "He told me that my performance in Munich did more for reducing the political tension during the Cold War between our two countries than the embassies were able to do in five years."

Teofilo Stevenson

The list of Olympic boxing gold medal winners who went on to become heavyweight champions of the world is a formidable one. It includes Muhammad Ali, Floyd Patterson, Joe Frazier and George Foreman. But the greatest Olympic heavyweight champion of them all never turned professional, and yet there are some who still believe he could have been the best. He was the Cuban sensation, Teofilo Stevenson.

At the 1972 Munich Olympics the 20-year-old, 6 foot 3½ inch Stevenson amazed the world with his powerful left jab and sledgehammer right hand.

Leading to the final he won all his bouts by technical knockout, and then had his hand raised high as Olympic champion without having to throw a punch in the championship bout. His opponent, Ion Alexe of Romania, injured himself in the semi-final and couldn't compete. Most observers called the injury a "merciful" one, for now Alexe could walk out of the ring instead of being carried out.

Four years later in Montreal, Stevenson continued his knockout string leading to the final. Again he would have to meet a Romanian, Mircea Simon, for the gold medal. Simon knew of Stevenson's reputation and stayed out of the tall Cuban's reach for more than two rounds. Finally Stevenson hit him with a blockbuster and before the slaughter could continue, the towel was thrown in, signifying that Simon had had enough. Stevenson had won his second gold medal.

Incredible financial offers from American promoters were thrown at Stevenson. His reply was always the same:

"I love my country and they love me. "I want to keep it this way."

At the 1980 Moscow Games Stevenson, now 28, again was easily the best in the world. His reputation had become such that opponents were thrilled to still be standing

94

at the end of three rounds as opposed to believing they had a chance to win the bout. In Moscow Stevenson won his third gold medal by winning a 4 to 1 decision over his Soviet opponent.

Stevenson had now tied László Papp of Hungary as the only man to win three successive gold medals in boxing. His chance at winning four were dashed when Cuba boycotted the 1984 Los Angeles Games.

Magnar Solberg

Grenoble, 1968; Sapporo, 1972   Norway

Magnar Solberg of Norway is perhaps the least known champion in the least known sport on the Olympic Winter program. . . the biathlon. The biathlon is one of the most demanding winter events — a combination of cross country skiing and rifle shooting. To win the event a fast skier must also be an accurate marksman. With each target missed, penalty minutes are added to the overall time of the cross country portion of the event. Thus the faster cross country skier can lose if he is not also an accurate marksman.

Magnar Solberg was a police officer in Trondheim. His superior officer, Martin Stokken, a silver medal winner in the cross country relay in 1952, noticed in police training that Solberg was calm under pressure, that Solberg did not flinch in dangerous situations. "Magnar had always been a good cross country skier and I realized he would be the perfect candidate for the biathlon because there was no danger that bothered him," said Stokken. "Martin Stokken became my best friend, my coach, my second father," said Solberg. "Some of his training methods were revolutionary, but I had complete trust in him."

As the 1968 Grenoble Olympics approached, Solberg, unknown even to his teammates, went through a rigorous training program. In the summer preceding the Games the physical training consisted of daily cross country runs combined with strength drills in the gymnasium. Stokken then devised a shooting schedule for the summer that would attempt to simulate the stress of being in actual competition in the winter.

"The most critical times during the competition are the few hundred meters before each shooting phase," says Solberg. "Then I had to concentrate on slowing down my pulse rate at least 50 beats in order to steady the rifle."

Stokken's plan for Solberg was torturous.

"I placed the target 50 meters away from an anthill," recalled Stokken. "Then Magnar would lie atop the anthill and shoot."

"The ants would crawl up my legs, all over my face, everywhere. It was awful. But Martin would not let me stop," said Solberg. "I did not believe it at the time but my ability to concentrate under those hot, painful conditions made the actual competition easy for me in the cold."

At the 1968 Grenoble Games Solberg was the only contestant to have a perfect "no miss" shooting score. This, combined with skiing the course in the second fastest time, was good enough to win him the gold medal. Four years later in Sapporo, using the same training methods, Solberg successfully defended his Olympic championship.

Irena Szewinska

Tokyo, 1964; Mexico City, 1968; Munich, 1972; Montreal, 1976   Poland

In the history of Olympic women's track and field there are familiar names known to all: legends such as Babe Didrikson, Fanny Blankers-Koen, Wilma Rudolph, Florence Griffith-Joyner and Jackie Joyner-Kersee, to name but a few. All have been multiple gold medal winners. But to many Olympic historians there is one woman who stands above all the rest. Her name is Irena Szewinska of Poland. In her homeland she is still known as "The Queen of the Track."

As an eighteen-year-old and competing under her maiden name of Irena Kirszenstein, she won a gold medal as a member of the Polish 4 x 100 relay team and silver medals in the 200 meters and long jump at the 1964 Tokyo Olympics.

In 1967, a year before the Mexico City Olympics, she married her longtime fiancé, Janusz Szewinska, a sports photographer. Though she was attending classes full-time as an economics major at Warsaw University, Irena made plans for the upcoming 1968 Mexico City Olympics. There she won a gold medal in the 200 meters and a bronze in the 100 meters.

Between the Mexico City Olympics and the 1972 Munich Games, she severely injured her ankle and it was slow to heal.

"The Munich Games were really the beginning of my second Olympic career," said Irena. "After my son Andrej was born in 1970 and then my injury, I couldn't train for about a year."

Nevertheless Irena made it to the 200 meter final. There she won the bronze medal, finishing behind Renate Stecher of East Germany and Raelene Boyle of Australia. Even the victorious Stecher, winner of both the 100 and 200 meters in Munich, was in awe of Szewinska.

"Irena was my idol when I was a youngster," said Stecher. "I had read of her great competitions in Tokyo and Mexico City but I never dreamed that one day I would be able to compete with her. Irena is the model for all sportsmen and sportswomen who aspire to greatness at the Olympic Games."

A year after the Munich Games, Irena and Janusz made two momentous decisions. Janusz would become her coach and she would compete in a new event — the 400 meters.

"Through many years of training, Irena had built up a tremendous amount of endurance," said Janusz. "Therefore it was logical that with her natural speed in the sprints combined with her endurance, the 400 meters would be an ideal distance for her."

Just two years after first attempting the 400 meters, Irena made history by becoming the first woman to run the distance under 50 seconds. Now she had one more world to conquer: an Olympic gold medal at the 1976 Montreal Games in her new event.

In her two preliminary heats, Irena barely qualified, finishing third and fourth. But she won her semi-final, setting an Olympic record. Her main opposition was expected from Christina Brehmer of East Germany, the only other woman at that time to run the distance under 50 seconds.

Brehmer started quickly and led down the backstretch, but Irena in third was in a good position to attack.

As they went into the last turn, though the lanes are staggered, it became apparent that Irena was fastest of all. When they straightened out for the stretch drive Irena increased her lead. At the finish Irena was almost ten meters in front of Christina Brehmer.

Twelve years after winning her first gold medal, the Polish national anthem was again played for 30-year-old Irena Szewinska. In four Olympic Games she had won at least one medal — in all, three gold, two silver and two bronze. Irena Szewinska fulfilled the finest attributes of the human spirit — talent, pride, courage and perhaps most of all, the ability to endure.

Dave Moorcroft

Los Angeles, 1984   Great Britain

On the afternoon of August 11, 1984, fourteen men lined up at the Los Angeles Coliseum for the final of the 5,000 meters. Based on their times and how they competed in their semi-finals, Said Aouita of Morocco, who had previously run the second fastest time ever, and John Walker of New Zealand, the Montreal 1,500 meters Olympic champion who had moved up to the 5,000 meters, were considered the men to beat.

However, many were predicting that Dave Moorcroft of Great Britain, who had held the 5,000 meter world record for two years, would end up the winner. In the summer of 1982 he broke the existing world record by more than five seconds and was less than a half second short of becoming the first man in history to run the distance under thirteen minutes.

In the two years leading to the Los Angeles Olympics, Moorcroft had been beset with crippling injuries. As he was about to step to the starting line in the Olympic 5,000 meters, he had not fully recovered from a stress fracture of the leg, a debilitating attack of hepatitis and a pelvic disorder that on certain days made it impossible to run.

"How do you feel, Dave?" I asked as the runners warmed up. I was at the starting line directing one of my eight camera crews covering the race.

"Not so good," he replied. "My stomach is acting up. It's painful, but I'll give it a try."

The race got under way and it immediately became evident that Moorcroft was in great pain. Sitting in the stands was Moorcroft's wife, Linda, carrying their two-year-old son, Paul.

"When I saw him warming up I knew something was amiss," recalled Linda Moorcroft. "He was dragging his leg and it was obvious to me that his pelvis had tilted again."

The race is twelve and a half times around the 400 meter track. After two laps Dave Moorcroft was in last place and running with painful, choppy strides.

"There was no way I could stay with the pace," recalled Moorcroft. "I thought of Linda watching in the stands and I knew what she was going through."

"As he fell further and further behind, I burst into tears," remembered Linda. "I was secretly hoping he would pull out of the race. But I knew he wouldn't. And I was praying that he wouldn't be lapped. I thought, please, please don't let him be lapped."

As the race moved into its final stages, Said Aouita of Morocco moved into the lead. Coming off the final turn Aouita's victory was assured. Some 30 meters in front of Aouita, but in actuality 370 meters behind, Moorcroft was in danger of being lapped.

"I didn't want to be lapped," recalled Moorcroft. "When you're the world record holder, regardless of the pain, you don't want to be lapped."

Moorcroft fought the pain and pushed on. He passed across the finish line a few feet in front of the victorious Aouita, but now must trudge his way around for his final 400 meters.

Aouita grabbed a Moroccan flag from an exuberant fan and took a victory lap. Moorcroft was still circling the track as the crowd roared its acclaim for the Moroccan. Very few people noticed that the world record holder, Dave Moorcroft, had still not completed the race.

When he finally crossed the finish line he was exhausted and in great pain.

Later I asked him why he did it, why he did not leave the track.

"I had never quit a race before and I was not going to start now at the Olympic Games," Moorcroft replied, seemingly surprised he would be asked such a question. "Once you quit, it's easy to do it again. I did not want to set a precedent for the future."

Two weeks later I called him in London and said I would like to come over and film his story. He politely said that he wanted to put the experience out of his thoughts, that they were the worst fifteen minutes of his lives.

I then told him that his dedication, courage and ability to endure would be an inspiration to millions of young people to use as a basis for conducting their life.

"Dave," I said, "you're a greater inspiration for all that is right in the human spirit than if you had won the race."

There were a few seconds of silence and I thought we had been disconnected. Then I could hear him sniffling, holding back the tears.

"Thank you very much," he said. "I would be honored to be part of your film."

Babe Didrikson

Los Angeles, 1932

On July 16, 1932, the women's AAU track and field championships were held at Northwestern University. The national championships had a dual purpose. They would also serve as the Olympic trials that would select the women's team that would compete at the Los Angeles Olympic Games less than a month away.

Twenty-one-year-old Mildred "Babe" Didrikson was a typist for the Employers Casualty Company team of Dallas, Texas. Entered in the championships, the term *team* was misleading. Didrikson was the only team member.

When the competition was over, Didrikson won five individual events — the high jump, shot put, javelin, 80 meter hurdles and a now obscure event, the baseball throw.

Olympic rules at the time permitted her to compete in only three events. Didrikson chose the javelin, 80 meter hurdles and high jump.

"I could have won a medal in five events if they'd let me," Didrikson would say before, during and after the Games.

On the first day of competition in Los Angeles, Babe won the javelin with her first toss. It was ten feet short of the world record of her teammate Nan Gindele, who came in fifth.

"I could have thrown it a lot farther if it hadn't slipped in my hand," Didrikson told reporters afterward. "At least ten feet farther, which would have given me the world record."

Four days later she was a finalist in the 80 meter hurdles. She became the favorite after tying the world record in her opening heat.

In the final her main opposition was expected to come from her teammate Evelyn Hall of Chicago.

The two ran neck and neck to the finish line and it was many minutes before the judges decided that Babe had won the race by two inches. Evelyn Hall never accepted the decision. For days afterward she would point to a red mark on her neck indicating the bruise was caused when she broke the tape.

The high jump was Babe's third and final event. Her main threat was teammate Jean Shiley, who tied Babe for first place in the Olympic trials.

They both cleared the world record height of 5 feet 5¾ inches, but the judges intervened with a strange decision. They declared that Babe's style of jumping was illegal, because her head preceded her body and legs over the bar. In those days the standard high jump technique required that the competitor's body over the bar before the head. The gold medal was awarded to Shiley and the silver to Didrikson.

"The judges were crazy," declared Babe afterward. "That's the way I jumped during the whole competition. If I was illegal on my last jump I was illegal on my first jump. So if they were right, I should have been disqualified from the beginning."

From her Olympic triumphs Babe went on to become one of the outstanding woman golfers of all time, and in 1950 was voted by the Associated Press the greatest woman athlete of the first half century.

USA-USSR Hockey

Lake Placid, 1980   USA/USSR

February 22, 1980, was George Washington's birthday. It was also the day that the young United States hockey team would face the heavily favored Soviet Union squad at the Lake Placid Olympic Games.

Even though both teams had gone through their first five games undefeated, the Americans were given little chance to win. Many believed that the Soviets were the best in the world — professional or amateur. Before the competition got under way the Soviets were seeded first in the rankings and the United States seventh.

"The Soviets had beaten us 10 to 3 in an exhibition a few days before the Olympics," remembered American coach Herb Brooks. "They were fantastic and deserved their ranking. I had little hope for a medal. I would have been very happy to have achieved a fourth place finish."

History was on the side of the Americans. In six previous Olympic competitions the Soviets had won five gold medals and one bronze. Their only loss came 20 years earlier at the 1960 Squaw Valley Olympics when an unheralded United States team defeated them in the semi-finals and then went on to defeat Czechoslovakia to win the gold medal. Now here in Lake Placid, patriotism was working on behalf of the Americans — it was Washington's birthday and the U.S. team was again playing the Soviets in a critical match on American soil. There was one more piece of hockey trivia that could be considered good or bad news. Coach Herb Brooks was the last man to be cut from the American squad that won the gold medals 20 years earlier.

The Americans played their hearts out for two periods, but still trailed the Soviets 3 to 2. United States goaltender Jim Craig kept the Americans in the game with superb save after save.

With less than nine minutes played in the third period the United States tied the game at 3 to 3. Then at the ten minute mark Captain Mike Eruzione let fly a blistering 30 footer that found the net and the United States led 4 to 3.

In the final ten minutes the Soviets attacked furiously, but goalie Craig was inspired in holding them off. The last few moments of the game will live forever as the last ten seconds were counted down to the final buzzer. "Do you believe in miracles?" screamed broadcaster Al Michaels, "Yes. . . . "

After the game the predominantly American crowd hovered outside the arena, walking up and down Lake Placid's Main Street. Almost on cue snowflakes began to fall and it signaled the spontaneous singing of "The Star Spangled Banner," "America the Beautiful," and "God Bless America."

The victory was so emotional many celebrating seemed unaware that the United States had to defeat Finland two days later to win the gold medal.

On Sunday morning, February 24, the United States met the Finns. As in the Soviet game, the United States trailed after two periods by one goal, 2 to 1. But nothing could stop the Americans in the third period. They scored three goals and won the game 4 to 2. Incredibly, the United States had won its second hockey gold medal twenty years apart — both times in the United States.

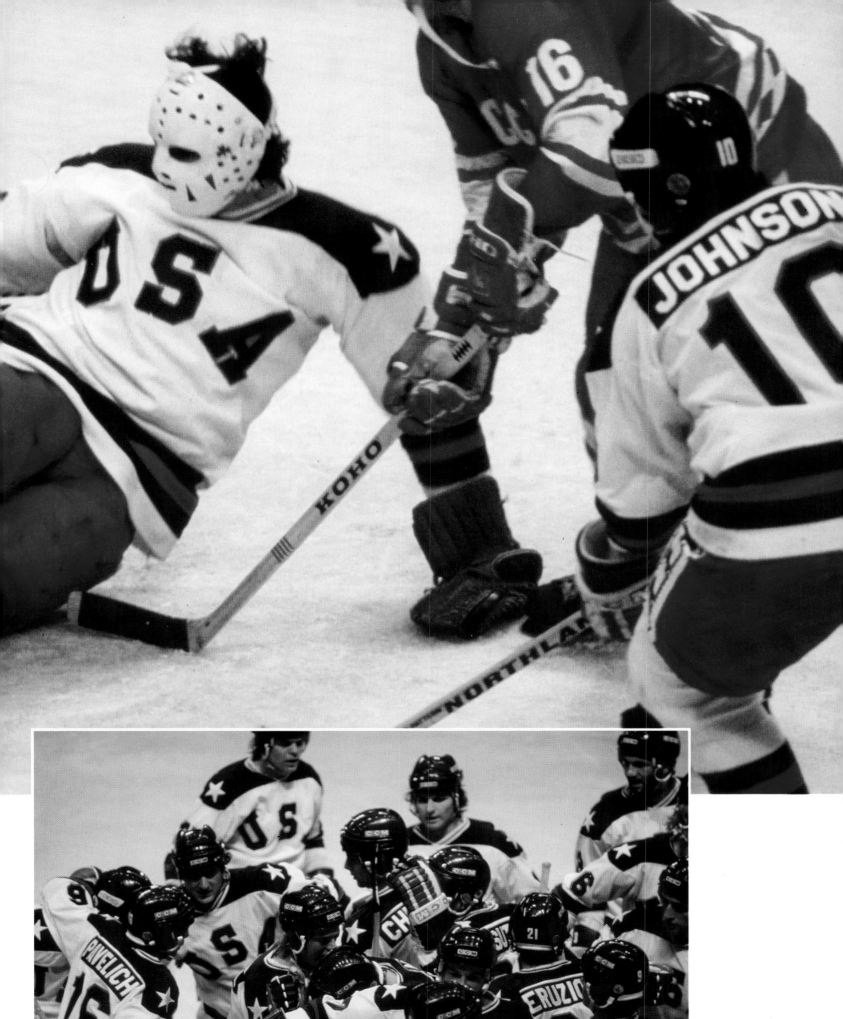

Frank Havens

Helsinki, 1952   United States

The United States eight-oared crew was considered a certainty to win the gold medal in this, the "classic" rowing event at the 1924 Paris Olympic Games.

One of the crew members was Benjamin Spock, who later would receive international acclaim as Dr. Spock, "the baby doctor," and author of child care books that have sold in the millions.

Another member of the prestigious U.S. Rowing Team was Bill Havens of Arlington, Virginia, who was one of America's great canoeing prospects. He was scheduled to compete in the single and four-man canoeing events in Paris and a favorite to stand on the victory podium.

A few months before the American team was to leave for Paris, Havens learned that his wife was going to give birth to their child at approximately the same time that the two-week Olympic competition would be taking place.

Bill Havens consulted his wife, family, friends and doctor. All of them assured him that he should go to Paris and be part of the team that was certain to win the gold medal and gain Olympic immortality. One must remember that the journey on the ship took almost two weeks over the seas to Paris.

After several days of soul searching Bill Havens made his decision. He would give up his place on the team and not go to the Olympics. He would be at his wife's bedside when their child was born. Four days after the Paris Games were over, on August 1, 1924, Frank Havens was born.

For years afterward Bill Havens was not certain he had made the right decision. He would often dream of standing atop the victory platform in Paris. It would take almost three decades before he realized he made the correct decision, for in the summer of 1952 he received a telegram from Helsinki, Finland, the scene of the Olympics. The telegram read:

"Dear Dad, Thanks for waiting around for me to get born in 1924. I'm coming home with the gold medal you should have won." It was signed, "Your loving son, Frank." Frank Havens had just won the gold medal in the singles 10,000 meters canoeing event.

Al Oerter

Melbourne, 1956; Rome, 1960; Tokyo, 1964; Mexico City, 1968

In the spring of 1976 we were holding weekly preview screenings for our then ten-part *Olympiad* series which would be televised nationally over PBS.

One of the weekly attendees to our screenings was 39-year-old Al Oerter, who won four successive gold medals in the discus in Melbourne (1956), Rome (1960), Tokyo (1964) and Mexico City (1968). Oerter had been retired for eight years.

One night after screening *The Incredible Five* in which Al Oerter's career was featured, the incomparable discus thrower invited me to dinner.

It was a social evening with no dramatic happenings during our light conversations. Suddenly a hesitant Oerter blurted out, "Bud, I want you to be the first one to know." Fearing that he would be telling me of some incurable disease or a tragic loss of a family member, I waited for him to continue.

"Bud. . . I'm going to make a comeback. I'm going to try and make the 1980 Olympic team. . . " he said without looking up. "Your films have given me Olympic fever."

"You'll be 43 years old," I said.

"I'm throwing better than I've ever thrown before," he said, knowing what my reply would be.

Al did try for the 1980 team. But that was the year of the United States boycott of the Moscow Games and a depressed Oerter went through the motions half-heartedly to try to make a team that wasn't going to Moscow. He finished fourth in the token Olympic trials but there is little doubt he would have qualified if the United States was going to compete in Moscow.

Al Oerter's career reads like a bad Hollywood movie. In each of his four Olympic appearances he was never the world record holder and never the favorite to win the Olympic gold medal. Even more, his introduction to the discus was, if not true, ridiculous.

"I was running the mile in high school," laughingly recalled Oerter. "One day I was finishing my workout when an errant discus came skipping in front of me from across the field where the discus throwers were working out. Rather than walk it back across the field I threw the discus back and it landed about 50 feet behind them. The next thing I knew was that the coach came running over and said, 'You're finished with the mile, you're now my discus thrower.'

After easily winning in Melbourne (1956) and Rome (1960), 28-year-old Oerter arrived in Tokyo for the 1964 Olympic Games not certain he would compete. A chronic cervical disc injury forced him to wear a neck brace. He

Al Oerter, the epitome of Olympic longevity, winning the gold in the discus at four successive Olympic Games. (Photos are chronological from left to right)

would also have to face Ludvik Danek of Czechoslovakia, the current world record holder and winner of 45 straight competitions.

But that was only the beginning of the trauma Oerter would have to face. About a week before the competition Oerter tore a cartilage in his rib cage in a fall while practicing on a wet field.

"I was bleeding internally. I couldn't move, I couldn't sleep and I consumed bottles of aspirin to alleviate the pain," Oerter recalled. "I went through ice treatments to minimize the bleeding and the doctors ordered me not to compete. But these are the Olympics and you die before you don't compete in the Olympics."

On the day of the competition Oerter received three shots of Novocain directly into the injury but it was little help. The pain was excruciating and after four rounds, Danek was in first place with a toss more than seven feet farther than Al's best effort. Even so, Oerter was in third place.

"I decided before the fifth round that it would be my last attempt. The pain was too much to take a sixth throw. I would go for broke in the fifth round," he remembered.

Al let the discus fly. Doubled up in pain, he never saw the discus land. The roar of the crowd forced him to look up. His toss was almost two feet farther than Danek's leading effort and good enough for an Olympic record. Danek's last throw could not match Oerter's effort. Al Oerter had won his third gold medal.

Four years later Al won his fourth gold medal in Mexico City at the age of 32 and retired an undefeated Olympic champion and the only athlete to win four consecutive gold medals in the same event in track and field.

Recently I had dinner with Al. The years had been kind to him. He looked as he did in his prime. When I asked him how things were, he replied with a smile.

"I won't try out for Atlanta but don't count me out for Sydney in the year 2000," he laughed.

How can you count Al out? He'll only be 64 years old.

Dawn Fraser

Melbourne, 1956; Rome, 1960; Tokyo, 1964

Australia

Australia's Dawn Fraser was one of a kind both in and out of the swimming pool. Fast talking, cocky, brash and independent, Dawn was constantly at odds with Australian officials for not adhering to the party line. Nevertheless, she was the finest swimmer of her day and to many the greatest ever, performing heroics that perhaps will never be duplicated.

"I love her," laughed America's Eleanor Holm, who was thrown off the 1936 Olympic team for drinking wine aboard the ship that was transporting the Olympians to the Berlin Olympics. "She reminds me a lot of me."

Dawn first gained international fame at the 1956 Melbourne Olympics when, before a home audience, she defeated her favored countrywoman Lorraine Crapp in the 100 meter freestyle, and in doing so created a world record. She followed this victory by winning a silver medal in the 400 meters.

Four years later at the 1960 Rome Olympics, unbeaten at the 100 meter distance since the Melbourne Games, she made Olympic history by becoming the first woman to win the event twice.

The next day Dawn got into a confrontation with teammates and Australian officials. The end result was that Dawn did not swim on the medley relay team.

Dawn continued to pile up victory after victory leading to the Tokyo 1964 Olympics and in the process became the first woman to swim the 100 meter distance under one minute.

Less than a year before the Tokyo Games, Dawn was in a tragic automobile accident that killed her mother. Dawn herself had a vertebral injury that threatened her career. Nevertheless, she recovered and made the Australian Olympic team for the third time.

Though she was in constant battles with officials, she was loved by the Australian people. She was "women's lib" long before the movement got under way and was the lone female representation of the happy-go-lucky, partygoing images that characterized her male counterparts. When Dawn was selected to carry the Australian flag in the Tokyo opening ceremonies, all of Australia rejoiced.

The 100 meter freestyle duel was the classic confrontation between the legendary 27-year-old Fraser and the new kid on the block, 15-year-old Sharon Stouder of the United States.

The race was close throughout and at 70 meters the two were even. But in one of the most dramatic finishes ever, Dawn touched the wall first, defeating the young American by two feet. Stouder, in defeat, gained glory by joining Dawn as the only other woman to swim the distance under 60 seconds.

With her victory, Dawn became the only swimmer, male or female, to win the same individual event three times, a record that still stands today.

The joy of victory was short-lived. After her triumph, Dawn made headlines when she led a group of teammates to the Emperor's Palace and successfully took home a Japanese flag from atop a flagpole.

Again all of Australia rejoiced after hearing of her antics, but Olympic officials were embarrassed and forced to make a public apology.

As punishment, Dawn was suspended for ten years and though the ban lasted only four years, at the age of 31 Dawn Fraser's career was over.

Norman Read
Melbourne, 1956

New Zealand

When sixteen-year-old Norman Read of Great Britain was a spectator at the 1948 London Olympics, he became fascinated with the victory of Sweden's John Ljunggren in the 50 kilometer walking race. He decided then that he wanted to become a "walker" and perhaps one day compete at the Olympics.

Read began training for the event, but soon realized that "walking events" were not popular in his native England, so he emigrated to New Zealand in 1954, two years before the scheduled 1956 Melbourne Olympic Games.

He continued his training and, as the Melbourne Games approached, Read wrote to the British Olympic team, asking to be named to the squad. The British AAA turned him down.

Depressed by the rejection, Read nevertheless continued to compete, and when he won important races in both Australia and New Zealand, he received an invitation from the New Zealand Olympic officials to join the team. Read jumped at the opportunity and very quickly he became a naturalized citizen of New Zealand.

The favorite in the race was Yevgeni Maskinskov of the Soviet Union, who led throughout most of the race. Read's strategy was to let the Soviet champion set the pace and then take over the lead with about ten kilometers to go. His plan worked to perfection.

"When I caught up to Maskinskov he had that blank look of surprise and perhaps shock," recalled Read. "At that point I think we both knew that the race was mine."

When Read entered the stadium thousands of New Zealanders in the stands were roaring their acclaim. When he crossed the finish line, arms raised high in triumph, he was more than two minutes ahead of the second place finisher, Maskinskov of the Soviet Union.

Read took a victory lap, then moved to the infield at the finish line to await the third place finisher. Read greeted the bronze medalist enthusiastically, for it was 37-year-old John Ljunggren of Sweden, whose victory eight years ago at the London Olympics was the impetus for Read's long, circuitous journey to the top step of the victory podium.

Afterward, during the press conference, a cynical Australian journalist took Read by surprise:

"Listen, mate," said the journalist, "what are you, a 'Pom' or a 'Kiwi'?" Without hesitation Read replied, "I'm a Pommy Kiwi and proud of it." The press room resounded with applause.

Norman Read, wearing number 10, cut a dashing figure for New Zealand in the 50 kilometer walking race in 1956.

114

John Davis London, 1948; Helsinki, 1952

United States

In the long list of American Olympic champions there was none greater and none more obscure than Brooklyn's John Davis. Whenever Davis is mentioned as an all-time Olympic great the reply is invariably, "John who?"

John Davis was heavyweight Olympic weightlifting champion in 1948 and 1952 and because of it earned the title of "the strongest man in the world."

Laughingly John would say, "I was born in the wrong country and at the wrong time."

An African American who competed in the pre-television era in a sport that received little attention in his native land, nevertheless John was revered, particularly in Europe, the Middle East, and many other countries throughout the world.

John won his first world championship in 1938 when he was seventeen and looked forward to becoming Olympic champion in the upcoming 1940 Games. But World War II intervened and both the 1940 and 1944 Olympics were canceled. John served with the Army in the South Pacific theater but nevertheless was able to win national championships in 1941, 1942 and 1943.

He was 27 when the Games were renewed in London in 1948 and arrived there undefeated in ten years. Davis easily won the heavyweight gold medal and when he returned to the United States there were moments when he thought his fortunes had changed.

Outside the United States, the world press greeted his victory with headlines and featured stories. The French called him L'Hercule Noir (Black Hercules) and offered him citizenship, a free home and financial freedom. Germany, Sweden, Spain, England and Egypt toasted his greatness in a manner usually reserved for their own champions.

But after returning to the United States he quickly learned that his victory was not a major happening to American sports fans. John believed in the purity of his sport and turned down all offers to exploit his great strength. Promoters called on him to become a professional wrestler but he would have none of it.

He did, however, accept an offer from the French Athletic Association to try to lift the famed Appollon wheels — actual railroad wheels weighing 365 pounds and joined together by a thick round axle. Before a cheering French audience, he became the third man in history to perform the feat.

Gold-medalist John Davis, center, watches teammate J. Bradford (silver) congratulate Argentina's H. Selvetti (bronze) after the heavyweight weightlifting event in the 1952 Games.

When he was 31 he went to Helsinki in 1952 to defend his Olympic title and there he gained a double honor. He not only won the gold medal but his victory was the deciding one in a 4 to 3 American triumph over the Soviet Union for the team championship.

Ironically in 1953 John finally received national attention by the American sports press. After fifteen years of never being beaten, John was finally defeated by his Olympic teammate, Norbert Schemansky who had won the middle heavyweight title at the 1952 Helsinki Games.

Of all the talks I had with John, the one I remember most was the time we were listening to baseball announcer Red Barber give a warm eulogy to a famous baseball player who had just died.

John shook his head and smiled. "If you're going to give someone flowers," he laughed, "make sure they're around to smell them." John died of cancer in 1984 after a lifetime of athletic greatness. But on very few occasions was he able to smell the flowers.

Eugenio Monti

Cortina d'Ampezzo, 1956; Innsbruck, 1964; Grenoble, 1968   Italy

Cortina d'Ampezzo, a village 4,000 feet high in the heart of the Italian Dolomite Mountains, was the site of the 1956 Winter Olympic Games. Cortina d'Ampezzo's most famous citizen is Eugenio Monti, perhaps the greatest bobsled driver in history.

"My first love has always been skiing," said Monti. "In 1951 I was Italy's national downhill champion and I had high expectations to win the downhill gold medal at the 1952 Oslo Olympics. But a few weeks before the Games I broke both my knees in a training accident and my competitive skiing career was over. My teammate, Zeno Colò, whom I defeated for the Italian championship, went on to win the Olympic gold medal."

Two years after his accident Monti entered a bobsled competition for "newcomers." His three friends who joined him decided that Monti should be the driver. "I was scared the first time down," he recalled, "but we won the race. I now knew I had a new sport."

When the 1956 Winter Olympics took place in Cortina d'Ampezzo, Monti had mastered the sport. He won silver medals in both the two-man and four-man events.

Because there was no bobsled run at the Squaw Valley 1960 Games, there was no competition scheduled, so Monti had to wait another four years for the 1964 Innsbruck Games. There he won two bronze medals. But he came away the most beloved and revered athlete of the Games.

In the two-man event the British team driven by Tony Nash was in second place after the first run. "When we got back to the top of the hill after our first run," recalled Tony Nash, "we found that our sled had a broken bolt on the rear axle. We were about to quit the competition. At the bottom of the hill Monti heard of our problem. Without hesitation Monti took the bolt out of his rear axle and sent it up to us. It was an incredible act of sportsmanship and friendship."

The British team went on to win the gold medal and Monti's sled finished in third place. For his magnificent deed Monti was awarded the De Coubertin Medal for Sportsmanship.

"There have been many stories written that say I was very generous in my assistance to Tony Nash. I do not believe that I did anything that Tony Nash would not have done for me or for anybody else in the competition," Monti says today. "Tony Nash did not win because I gave him a bolt. Tony Nash won because he was the best driver and deserved to win."

Four years later at the 1968 Grenoble Games Eugenio Monti reached the pinnacle of his career. He won both the two-man and four-man events, giving him an Olympic total of two gold, two silver and two bronze medals.

When Monti retired perhaps the greatest tribute was given him by Tony Nash, the man he aided at the 1964 Innsbruck Games.

"Like any in a major sport, you get your heroes," said Nash. "Monti was a hero both in and out of competition. He would make mistakes but he would gain time making them. I don't know how he did it. I wish to heaven I knew. I'd have been a better bobsledder for it."

Brian Orser & Brian Boitano

Calgary, 1988
Canada/United States

On the evening of February 20, 1988, more than 19,000 spectators packed the Olympic Saddledome in Calgary to witness the final phase of the men's figure skating championship — the climax of a three-day competition.

Although 24 men were entered, for more than a year it was well known that the battle for the gold medal was going to be between but two — Brian Orser of Canada, the 1987 world champion and silver medalist at the 1984 Sarajevo Olympics, and Brian Boitano of the United States, the 1986 world champion who finished fifth in Sarajevo four years earlier.

Although they were close friends, the press throughout the world heralded the meeting as the Battle of the Brians.

Before the evening began, Boitano led Orser by two-tenths of a point — the tabulations after the compulsory figures and short programs constituting 50% of the final total score. On this night they would each skate a four-and-a-half-minute long program for the final 50% of the total score.

As is custom with elite skaters, Boitano and Orser would be among the last six skaters to perform. . . Boitano will be the 19th skater and Orser 21st.

Boitano skated spectacularly but Orser was not a witness to it.

"When Brian Boitano was doing his long program I was backstage mentally going through my own performance," Orser remembered. "I could hear his music and I could hear the cheers of the crowd so I knew he had skated well. However, I was more or less oblivious to what was going on because of my own concentration."

A tremendous roar from his countrymen greeted Orser as he stepped onto the ice. Though Boitano's marks were very high, there was still room for Orser to win the gold medal. However, Orser knew he must skate the "perfect" program to win top honors. The tension had reached Orser's mother sitting in the stands. She left her seat and would not return until her son's performance was over. She was not alone.

"I did not want to watch him," said Boitano. "I went backstage and sat in the bathroom and listened to music on my Walkman. I waited five minutes before leaving the bath-

room, for I wanted his performance to be over. When I took off my earphones, I heard the last judge gave him a perfect 6, so I resigned myself to second place."

The two Brians found out the result in different ways.

"My teammate, Christopher Bowman, came running over to me with a big smile," remembered Boitano, "and he was nodding his head up and down. Since he was a practical joker, I wasn't sure. Then I said, 'Christopher, if you're playing a joke on me it's the meanest thing you've ever done.' And Christopher said, 'It's no joke. . . You've Won!'"

Orser was watching the monitor alongside the Canadian broadcasters.

"I looked at the monitor, then at my Canadian broadcaster friends who were giving the results," remembered Orser. "I saw the bleak look on their faces. Then they shook their heads, 'No,' and I knew that I didn't win."

Of the nine judges, the victory was given to Boitano by a 5 to 4 decision — the closest finish in the history of men's figure skating.

"I dreamed before the Games that I would be standing on the top step of the podium hearing the Canadian national anthem," said Orser years later with tears swelling again in his eyes. "It just didn't happen as I dreamed."

Betty Robinson

Amsterdam, 1928; Berlin, 1936

United States

If a fiction writer handed in a screenplay on Betty Robinson's life, it would be greeted unanimously with the words, "Nobody will believe it."

Betty Robinson was a legitimate "first" — the first female track gold medal winner in Olympic history.

Five track and field events for women were introduced at the 1928 Amsterdam Games — the 100 meters, 800 meters, 4 x 100 relay, discus and high jump. The first women's track event scheduled was the 100 meters. Three Canadian, two German and one American made it to the final. The lone American was sixteen-year-old Betty Robinson, a high school student from Illinois. The field was cut down to four when two women, one Canadian and one German, were disqualified for two false starts. Nevertheless Fanny Rosenfeld of Canada was still in the race and she was still the overwhelming favorite. Betty Robinson was given little chance. How she got here would read like pure fiction if it had not been documented as fact.

"I was running for the train that took me to school one day," recalled Robinson. "The coach of the track team watched out of the window of the train as I caught up to it and suggested that I should develop my talent. Till then I didn't even know there were women's races."

History was made on July 31, 1928, when Betty was declared the winner over Fanny Rosenfeld in a close finish.

A few days later Betty ran the anchor leg on the 4 x 100 relay team that came in second behind the Canadians. In two events Betty Robinson had won a gold and a silver medal. She now looked forward to competing in the 1932 Games when, at age 20, she would be in her prime.

The year before the 1932 Games tragedy struck. Betty was in an airplane accident and was unconscious for almost two months, suffering severe injuries to her arm, leg and head. She of course missed the 1932 Olympics.

Though she could not bend her knee down "on the mark," Betty continued her rehabilitation and two years after the accident was back running. Incredibly, she was named to run on the United States 4 x 100 relay team that was going to compete in the 1936 Berlin Olympics.

The overwhelming favorite to win was the star-studded German team that set a world record in a preliminary heat. The German team was ten meters faster than the American team, and the most the Americans could logically hope for was the silver medal.

Betty Robinson was assigned the third leg and would hand the baton off to Helen Stephens, the 100 meter gold medal winner.

"The Germans were about ten meters ahead when I was about to pass the baton to Helen," said Robinson, "but then I saw the German girl throw her arms to her head and break down crying. She had dropped the baton."

Helen Stephens went on to win the gold medal and Betty Robinson had won her second gold medal.

Viktor Saneyev

Mexico City, 1968; Munich, 1972; Montreal, 1976; Moscow, 1980   USSR

When discus thrower Al Oerter of the United States won his event at the 1968 Mexico City Olympics, he created a record that seemingly would never be duplicated in track and field competition. Oerter's victory was his fourth successive triumph, following victories at the 1956 Melbourne, 1960 Rome and 1964 Tokyo Games.

While Oerter won his fourth gold medal with comparative ease, a thrilling competition took place in triple jump (formerly the hop, step and jump). There the previous world record was broken nine times before a winner finally was crowned. That honor went to Viktor Saneyev of the Soviet Union. No one knew then that Saneyev would threaten Oerter's feat.

"It was an incredible competition," remembered Saneyev. "It seems that every time someone jumped, a world record was created. Finally, on my sixth and last attempt, the world record was broken for the ninth time and I won the gold medal."

Four years later in Munich an injured Saneyev knew that he would have to win early or go home in defeat. His first leap was tremendous and it held up during the entire competition. Saneyev had won his second gold medal.

As the 1976 Montreal Games approached, a new triple jump star appeared. He was Joao Oliveira of Brazil.

"I did not know what to expect in Montreal," said Saneyev. "In the triple jump world records are broken by an infinitesimal part of an inch. Oliveira came into the Games a year after he broke my world record by *almost a foot and a half.*"

But Oliveira could not match his world record performance. His best effort could earn him only the bronze medal. Viktor Saneyev again came through with a magnificent fifth round leap to overcome the surprise performance of America's James Butts, who to that point was in the lead. Viktor Saneyev had won his third gold medal.

"I would now try to end my career with another victory before my countrymen at the 1980 Moscow Games," said Saneyev.

Saneyev trailed his teammate Jaak Uudmae by almost eleven inches as he prepared for his sixth and final jump in Moscow.

"The crowd was cheering me as I got ready for my final attempt. I was not in the best of condition, but the crowd urged me on for one final effort," said Saneyev.

When Saneyev landed, many in the crowd believed he had done it. His name resounded through the stadium. He failed by a little more than four inches.

"I knew I fell short, but the crowd was magnificent," said Saneyev. "My teammate, Jaak Uudmae, jumped brilliantly and deserved to win. For me it was a great honor to end my career with three gold medals and one silver."

So today, Al Oerter still remains the only athlete to win four successive gold medals in track and field.

Lindy Remigino Helsinki, 1952

When the six finalists for the 100 meter final lined up at the 1952 Helsinki Olympics most experts predicted that it would be a duel between the two semifinal winners, McDonald Bailey of Great Britain and Herb McKenley of Jamaica. Twenty-one-year-old Lindy Remigino of the United States had little hope of winning. "I thought I might sneak in for the bronze," he still smiles, thinking about it today.

Remigino's road to Helsinki gave no great indications he would battle for the gold medal. Remigino finished second in the United States Olympic trials, but he would be up against faster runners from around the world in Helsinki.

"Just before the Olympic final Herb McKenley came into the dressing room," recalled Remigino, "and said 'Bailey looks scared stiff, Lindy. I think it's gonna be between you and me.' That perked me up a bit. Here's the guy that most everyone picks to win and he comes in and talks to me."

The race was the closest in Olympic history, four men hitting the tape simultaneously. "I went up to Herb and congratulated him because I thought he had won," said Remigino.

"Lindy came over to me and congratulated me on the victory," recalled McKenley, "and the judges all pointed to

In background: Lindy Remigino (number 981) wins the 100 meter final, trailed closely by Herb McKenley of Jamaica (number 295).

me as the winner, but we had to wait for the official photograph to confirm it."

"For about 20 minutes there was no official announcement," said Remigino. "But everyone was congratulating Herb and all the talk was that he had won and maybe I was second or third, so close was the finish."

The thousands in the stands were all waiting for the scoreboard to present the results. Finally a Finnish official walked over to Remigino, still standing at the finish line. "Mr. Remigino," said the official, "I think you have won the gold medal. . . "

"Suddenly the crowd was cheering," said Remigino. "I looked at the scoreboard and it was incredible. My name was first followed by McKenley. Bailey of Great Britain was third and my teammate, Dean Smith, fourth. But we were all timed in 10.4."

"It was so close between Lindy and me," said McKenley. "I looked at the photo and thought I had won, but then they showed me Lindy's shoulder had crossed the line first."

A few days later Remigino ran the third leg on the victorious United States 4 x 100 relay team — a second gold medal for a man who wasn't even supposed to make the team.

Inset: The U.S.A.'s victorious 4 x 100 meter relay team (left to right), Dillard, Remigino, Stanfield and Smith.

Alberto Tomba   Lillehammer, 1994   Italy

It is rare that an athlete will be remembered more in defeat than in victory. Such was the case with Italy's Alberto Tomba.

Leading to the 1994 Lillehammer Games the 27-year-old Tomba had become the most publicized alpine skier in competition. His own exploits off the slopes got even more attention than his magnificent performances in world and Olympic competition.

At the 1988 Calgary Olympics, 21-year-old Tomba came from virtual obscurity to win both the slalom and giant slalom events. His victory parties were as widely covered as his victories.

"It is true that I gave a party to celebrate my victories," smiles Tomba today. "But what people do not know is I always give parties. I would have had a big party even if I had lost."

Four years later in Albertville the 25-year-old Tomba made Olympic history when he again won the giant slalom, to become the only alpine skier to win gold medals in the same event in consecutive Olympics.

A few days later he won the silver in the slalom, missing the gold by .28 of a second.

As the 1994 Lillehammer Games approached, stories circulated in Italy that he was not training well and was out of shape.

"You know, when I go to other countries, everyone likes me and they write nice things about me," said Tomba. "But at home it is different. Because every time I do something wrong, they write about it. Even when I do something right, they make it seem like it is wrong."

Sixty-one men were entered in the Lillehammer giant slalom. Regardless of the press reports, Tomba was considered by many to be the favorite to win his third straight giant slalom.

Tomba's performance gave credibility to the pre-Olympic reports. After the first run he was in thirteenth place, more than a second behind the leader. But to the Tomba "faithful" their champion could easily make this up on the second run.

Tomba went all out, but he missed the third gate from the finish and was disqualified.

Four days later, by the luck of the draw, Tomba was the first man off in the slalom. When the 60th skier had finished the first run, Tomba was in 12th place, almost two seconds behind the leader.

"I did not think there was a chance for a medal," said Tomba. "There were eleven skiers in front of me with faster first round times. If there were only three or four I had to beat, maybe there would be a chance. But I must try my best. This might be my last Olympic race."

Tomba's second run was breathtaking — the only man to go the distance under one minute. His superb effort put incredible pressure on the eleven men who were in front of him after the first round.

Tomba watched his opposition from the bottom of the hill. One by one they failed to finish the course or their cumulative times were slower than Tomba's. Amazingly, Tomba's magnificent second run had put him in the lead with only one skier left that can beat him — Thomas Stangassinger of Austria, the leader after the first round.

Stangassinger skied well. He knew he had an almost two second lead over Tomba. When he crossed the finish line, he raised his arms in victory. He was more than a second and a half slower than Tomba, but his combined total after the two runs gave him the victory by fifteen-

hundredths of a second. Tomba, smiling happily, was the first one to greet the Olympic champion.

"It was very exciting to go from twelfth place to second," said Tomba. "And the fact that I won medals at three Olympic Games is something that has never been done in my sport. What more could I ask?"

Afterward one columnist wrote, "Alberto's second run brought back glories of the past. In less than one minute he left a legacy for all those who will follow. The words, 'A man is not finished when he is defeated. He is only finished when he leaves the arena.'"

Peter Vidmar

Los Angeles, 1984

On the evening of August 2, 1984, at the Los Angeles Olympic Games the battle for the men's individual all-around gymnastic title was not decided until the last apparatus. After five of the six apparatus had been contested, Koji Gushiken of Japan was in first place, leading America's Peter Vidmar by twenty-five-thousandths of a point.

All the contestants had to compete in six apparatus — the high bar, vault, rings, pommel horse, parallel bars and floor exercise. So that all the apparatus can be contested simultaneously, the 36 finalists were placed in six groups of six. Gushiken and Vidmar werein different groups. Gushiken's last apparatus was the floor exercise while Vidmar would compete in the parallel bars.

Earlier that morning of the finals Vidmar, a devout Mormon, went to Pauley Pavilion on the UCLA campus for one final practice session.

"I thought I was going to be alone," said Vidmar. "But in the corner was Koji Gushiken. He was reading out loud from what I believed to be a religious book."

"When I was in high school my teacher gave me a book which I always keep with me," said Gushiken. "It is entitled *The Creation of Life Worth Living*. My teacher said the teachings in the book would help me become the greatest gymnast in the world. The main message is simple. 'Look up to ideals, but do not run away from reality.' Just before I perform I speak the words 'Topa, Topa, Topa' which means, 'Concentrate and perfect yourself, and you will break through the barriers.'"

"Finally, Koji stood up and bowed toward one of the corners," recalled Vidmar. "Then he saw me and was very surprised. Then he said, 'Oh, Vidmar'. . . and we spoke in sign language. . . and we both knew we were wishing each other good luck."

There was additional drama for the final confrontation between Gushiken and Vidmar. Observing the competition from a front row seat assigned to an Official Film camera crew was Vidmar's wife, Donna. A year before the Games I hired her as a production assistant to work on our official film of the Los Angeles Games, *16 Days of Glory*.

Donna Vidmar was an accomplished gymnast. She also had the uncanny skill of being able to calculate the scoring with pen and paper — far quicker than the electronic technology that flashed the totals to the spectators in the arena.

"I was right by the parallel bars waiting for Peter to compete," said Donna. "Gushiken had just completed his floor exercise and the judges gave him a 9.90. I just wanted to rush down to the floor and tell Peter that he needed a 9.95 on the parallel bars to win the gold medal. But then I figured Peter knew that."

"I absolutely did not keep track of where I stood and what I needed to win," said Vidmar afterward. "I knew where Donna was sitting but I was so involved in the competition we never made eye contact."

Vidmar's routine was spectacular, but he took a slight hop upon landing. Nevertheless, he smiled brightly as if in triumph.

"I knew that the little hop on the dismount would mean deductions," said Donna. "I expected he would receive a 9.90, which would give him the silver medal. It was very sad and I started to cry. I looked to Peter and he was still smiling. But I already knew that he had lost the gold medal." She was right.

Vidmar, however, had his moment of glory. He was one of the U.S. gymnasts that won the team title. . . the first ever gold medal won by an American gymnastics team in 80 years.

Peter Snell
Rome, 1960; Tokyo, 1964

New Zealand

Every Sunday New Zealand's legendary track coach, Arthur Lydiard, would take his runners to the tortuous Waitakere Range where they would train over a rugged 20 mile course. Peter Snell was one of the long list of history-making New Zealand runners who trained under Lydiard.

"Arthur had an amazing sort of psychology," recalled Snell. "If we complained, he would say, 'Look, once you get to the stage where you can run 20 miles hard, come back and feel as though you can do it again, then you'll be right for anyone in the world, no matter what the distance.'" Lydiard's prophecy was fulfilled in the person of Peter Snell, who today is called by many the greatest Olympic middle distance champion ever.

Roger Moens, Belgium's world record holder, came off the last turn of the Rome Olympics 800 meter final in the lead.

"There was no one in front of me," recalled Moens. "As I moved down the stretch I closed my eyes and said to myself, 'I am the Olympic champion.' As the finish line approached I again closed my eyes and said to myself, 'Roger, it is certain. You are the Olympic champion!' Then a black uniform flashed by me. It was Peter Snell." A few moments later Snell crossed the finish line, Olympic champion.

Before the 1960 Rome Olympics very few people outside of New Zealand had ever heard of Peter Snell.

"I considered myself rather fortunate to be on the team," recalled Snell. "My best time leading to Rome was about 25th in the world. I thought I would be one of the finalists but quite frankly the idea of winning the gold medal never entered by mind."

In the four years between the Rome and Tokyo Games, Snell became the world record holder in both the 800 meters and mile run, the equivalent of the Olympic 1,500 meters. But leading to Tokyo, his 800 meter performances were suspect. Many in the world press claimed he had peaked in Rome. But some experts still gave him considerable support in the 1,500 meters.

"Prior to Tokyo I had thoughts of retirement," recalled Snell. "But then I decided that this would be my last big effort. I would run in both the 800 and 1,500 meters."

At the opening ceremonies the 26-year-old Snell was given the honor of carrying the New Zealand flag.

A few days later he demolished the 800 meter world class field to win his second successive gold medal. Now he would attempt the 1,500 meters. No athlete had won both races since Great Britain's Albert Hill performed that feat almost a half century earlier at the 1920 Antwerp Games.

In the 1,500 meter final the crowd was amazed to see two all-black New Zealand uniforms among the leaders. Seeing Peter Snell up front was no surprise but he was joined by his countryman John Davies. Incredibly, with one lap to go Davies was in the lead. But like all his opponents, he was waiting for Snell to make his move.

"I was still in the lead and I began to dream that maybe a miracle would occur," recalled Davies. "Then it happened. This black 'singlet,' the same as mine, went zooming past me. And there were these great bulky muscles of Snell's legs going down the track away from me and he was actually tearing great big chunks of cinders out of the track. With the power that he was generating, my dream was over. So was everybody else's." Snell had completed the 800/1,500 double.

A few years back I was commissioned to write an article for the *Los Angeles Times* about an 800 meter "dream race" that would include every Olympic and world record holder of the 20th century. The article would be based on the selection of 20 of the world's leading track and field experts, both coaches and press. The ballot was secret. All 20 selected Peter Snell as the winner.

132

Tenley Albright

Cortina d'Ampezzo, 1956   United States

Dr. Tenley Albright is a prominent surgeon living in Boston. Dr. Tenley Albright is even more famous as one of the world's great figure skating champions, whose career is one of the most dramatic and courageous in the history of the sport.

When she was eleven, she contracted polio. "I was not completely paralyzed, but I did not have use of my leg, back and neck," recalled Albright. "I did get cured and was able to skate, but my parents told me not to be surprised if the other kids wouldn't play with me, fearing they might catch polio."

At the 1952 Olympics in Oslo, sixteen-year-old Tenley Albright won the women's figure skating silver medal. Her free skating performance was brilliant and experts predicted certain victory four years later at the 1956 Games in Cortina d'Ampezzo. It would be a first. No American woman had ever won the Olympic figure skating gold medal.

A few weeks before the Cortina Games were to begin, tragedy struck Tenley during a practice session. "I fell and slashed my right leg with the blade of my left skate," remembered Tenley. "The cut was a jagged one, very bloody and reached the bone. Fortunately it didn't break any of the bone."

Tenley placed a call to her father in Boston, Dr. Hollis Albright, who immediately flew to Cortina. "Dad patched me up good," recalled Tenley. "But on the day of the competition I was worried. My leg was stiff and my ankle was all taped up."

Tenley Albright had a slight lead over her teammate Carol Heiss after the compulsory exercises, which in 1956 represented 60% of the total score. Now as the freestyle got under way, Tenley would have to test her leg with intricate jumps and spins.

"I was skating to 'The Bacarolle' from the *Tales of Hoffman*," smiled Tenley, remembering it as if it were yesterday. "Suddenly, almost as if orchestrated, the audience began to sing the words, and their voices just thrilled me. I forgot about the injury and just skated. But I must confess the chills were going up and down my spine."

That night the victory ceremony took place and Tenley Albright stood on the top step of the podium.

"It was a dark, cold night and there were lights all over the surrounding mountains," says Tenley. "Then they announced my name on the loudspeakers, which resounded through the valley. Then they raised the American flag and I got the biggest surprise. I was waiting for them to play 'The Star Spangled Banner.' But instead they began to play 'My Country 'Tis of Thee.' It was beautiful, but I still don't know why they didn't play 'The Star Spangled Banner.'"

Paavo Yrjola

Antwerp, 1920; Paris, 1924; Amsterdam, 1928   Finland ✚

The winner of the Olympic decathlon is rewarded with the title of "the finest all-around athlete in the world." Ever since the event was introduced to the Olympics at the 1912 Stockholm Games when Jim Thorpe defeated the second place finisher by nearly 700 points, the ten event decathlon has become one of the glamour events of the track and field competition. Bob Mathias, Bill Toomey, Milt Campbell, Rafer Johnson, Bruce Jenner and Daley Thompson are just some of the great athletes who have stood on the top step of the victory podium. But perhaps the most unknown and obscure "great one" was Paavo Yrjola of Finland — the 1928 decathlon winner in Amsterdam.

Yrjola was the least known of the Flying Finns who dominated the distance running at the Paris 1924 Olympics. He finished ninth in the 1924 decathlon, but after the Games began a streak of world record performances that climaxed with a magnificent Olympic victory in Amsterdam in 1928.

Paavo Yrjola was a self-made decathlete. He lived, worked and trained on his family farm about 80 miles outside of Finland's capital city of Helsinki.

"I was able to practice in the throwing events with a real javelin, discus and shot put," said Yrjola. "I would throw them as far as I could, and then I would walk to where they landed. I did not have a tape measure, so I only knew the approximate distance."

Yrjola's training in the other events was more complex.

"I cut down some trees on my farm and made a pole so I could practice the pole vault," remembered Yrjola. "I also made my own hurdles, but I wasn't sure they were always the right height. I usually tried to make the hurdles taller than under race conditions. That made it easier for me to clear them during a race."

Continuing his narrative, Yrjola explained how he practiced for the running part of the decathlon.

"I calculated that the big rock out there was about 200 meters from where we are standing," Yrjola said, pointing with a sweep of his hand. "Then I would run to the rock and then run back for the 400 meters and 1,500 meters training. I must have miscalculated my distances, for running in the Olympics seemed a lot shorter than the distance I was running on my farm."

At the end of our meeting in 1975 when Yrjola was 73, the Finnish champion said unemotionally, "I was not surprised that I won the decathlon in 1928 and in doing so broke my own world record. Since I trained alone in 1928 nobody knew how well I was doing. But I bought as many newspapers as I could and found out how my opponents were doing. But they didn't know how I was doing leading to the Olympics, so when I got to Amsterdam I was certain that I would win."

Derek Redmond

Barcelona, 1992   Great Britain

At 7:35 p.m. on the evening of August 3, 1992, eight men lined up for the first semi-final of the 400 meters at the Barcelona Olympics. The first four finishers in each semi-final would qualify for the final scheduled for two days later.

The favorite in the first semi was Steve Lewis of the United States, the defending Olympic champion from the Seoul Olympics four years earlier. One of the men expected to challenge Lewis and given a good chance to win one of the medals was Derek Redmond of Great Britain. Redmond, winning both his preliminary heats, was expected to easily make it to the final.

Leading to Barcelona, Redmond's career was plagued with injuries. At the 1988 Seoul Games, Redmond was given a chance at winning a medal, but he never got to the starting line. Just before his qualifying race, he had to withdraw because of a pulled Achilles tendon. Later, other injuries forced him to miss

major competitions, including the European championships and the Commonwealth Games.

However, at the 1991 Tokyo world championships, Redmond gained international fame, running the second leg of the 4 x 400 British relay team that defeated the heavily favored foursome from the United States.

Sitting in the stands in Barcelona was Jim Redmond, Derek's father and most ardent supporter.

"I saw him on the morning of the race," recalled Jim Redmond. "He was in marvelous shape, in good spirits. He was full of confidence and seemed to be the man they would have to beat."

At the start of the race Redmond got off quickly in lane five and began to make up the stagger on the runners to his right in lanes six, seven and eight. He could not see Steve Lewis, who was to his left in lane three.

"I couldn't believe I was going so fast," recalled Redmond. "I was running so easily it didn't appear to me I was going that fast."

The runner had gone more than 150 meters, moving down the backstretch toward the halfway point.

"I was getting ready to make my turn around the bend when suddenly I heard a funny 'pop,'" said Redmond. He had torn a hamstring in his right leg. Sitting in the stands, Jim Redmond was in shock.

"I couldn't believe it," recalled Jim Redmond. "I knew it was Derek but I didn't want to believe it."

Derek Redmond was in pain, motionless at the spot where he had suffered the injury. The other seven runners finished the race but now all eyes were on the helpless Redmond. Suddenly, a man appeared on the track, hurrying to the injured runner. He ran past medics who were carrying a stretcher. It was Jim Redmond, trying to catch up to his son. Finally, Jim Redmond reached his son trying to finish the race.

"The first thing Dad said as he put his arms around me was, 'Look, you don't have to do this.' And I told him, 'Yes, I do.' And he said, 'Well, if you're going to finish this race, we'll finish it together.'"

There, at the Barcelona Olympic stadium, unfolded one of the most memorable scenes in the history of the Olympic Games: a son being helped by his father making their way around the track to the finish line. And in defeat gaining as much glory as if he had won.

Sohn Kee-Chung Berlin, 1936 Korea

On August 9, 1936, 56 runners lined up for the start of the 26 mile, 385 yard marathon, the classic event in track and field, at the Berlin Olympic Games. The favorite in the race was Juan Zabala of Argentina, the defending champion from the 1932 Los Angeles Olympics.

In the early stages of the race Zabala took the lead. One of the runners trailing Zabala was Kitei Son of Japan. Son was born in Korea of Korean parents four years after his country was annexed by Japan. The only way he could compete in the Berlin Olympics was as a member of the Japanese team.

Kitei Son was not happy running under the Japanese flag and having to wear the Rising Sun emblem on his white shirt.

A fervent nationalist who deplored the Japanese occupation of his homeland, Kitei Son did everything short of holding a press conference to let the world know his true feelings.

Before the Games got under way he signed the official Olympic register with his Korean name, Sohn Kee-Chung. To emphasize the point he drew a small flag of Korea beside his name. One of the athletes he befriended was the legendary American marathoner, John Kelly.

"He was very emphatic," Kelly recalled decades later. "He would tell everybody he was not Japanese. That he was Korean. He would keep telling everyone, 'Me Korean. . . not Japanese.'"

As the 1936 Berlin marathon progressed, Zabala was still in the lead at the halfway mark, but he was faltering badly. Kitei Son and Great Britain's Ernest Harper, in second and third place, stalked the Argentine champion.

With twelve kilometers in the race, Kitei Son and Harper passed the tiring Zabala. Four kilometers later, Zabala collapsed and had to retire from the race. Now in third place was Shoryu Nan of Japan, who, like Kitei Son, was a Korean compatriot and forced to run under the same conditions. His Korean name was Nam Sung-Yong.

The rest of the race was not in doubt. Kitei Son

entered the stadium and was cheered by spectators in the stands who didn't realize the true story of the new Olympic marathon champion.

Two minutes later Ernest Harper of Great Britain entered the stadium and moved to the finish line. But an even greater applause greeted Shoryu Nan from the spectators, who believed the Japanese runners had won the gold and bronze medals.

"When they played the Japanese national anthem after my victory, I bowed my head," recalled Sohn Kee-Chung more than a half century later.

The climax to Sohn Kee-Chung's marathon victory in 1936 took place 52 years later at the opening day ceremonies of the Seoul Olympic Games on September 17, 1988. Then more than 70,000 spectators roared their acclaim. For entering the stadium carrying the flame that would burn throughout the Games was 76-year-old Sohn Kee-Chung. The crowd rose in tribute. Sohn Kee-Chung's lifetime journey for Olympic immortality as a Korean was now confirmed.

Vladimir Smirnov

Twenty-nine-year-old Vladimir Smirnov of Kazakhstan for years had stood in the shadow of the Norwegian cross country ski superstars. But Smirnov's rivalry with a host of Norwegians, his close friendship with Norway's legendary Vegard Ulvang and his graciousness in defeat had endeared him to all of Norway. At the Lillehammer 1994 Games, though he skied for Kazakhstan, Norwegians considered him one of their own.

"Vegard Ulvang is my best friend. We have had many trips and adventures together," says Smirnov. "And the Norwegian people. There is so much love. They yell, 'Smirnov, Smirnov, Smirnov whether I win or lose."

Smirnov's road to Lillehammer was a unique one. Six years earlier he competed at the Calgary Games representing the Soviet Union and won two silver and one bronze. Four years later in Albertville, he was part of the Unified Team of former Soviet republics but did not win any medals. It was in Albertville that his friends from Norway, Ulvang and Bjorn Daehlie, each won three gold medals. Now here in Lillehammer, Smirnov represented Kazakhstan, the land of his birth.

Though Ulvang was his closest friend, Smirnov's most dramatic battles have been with Bjorn Daehlie which reached their most thrilling moment at the 1993 world championships in Falun, Sweden. Then, in the combined pursuit event, they raced within inches of each other throughout the entire race and crossed the finish line together. Afterward Smirnov's name appeared first on the scoreboard, then Daehlie's. Both were given the same time.

"Everyone congratulated me, even Daehlie," remembers Smirnov. "Then about ten minutes later they changed their decision after viewing the video-tape, and I was in second place."

"I was sad for a few days," says Smirnov, "but then something happened that was difficult to believe. I received hundreds of letters from people in Norway, many from small children. Some of the letters from children had 'paper' gold medals attached, saying that I was a fine sportsman and that both of us should have received gold medals."

At the Lillehammer Games, Smirnov continued to chase the Norwegians. He finished tenth in the 30K won by Norway's Thomas Alsgaard. In the combined pursuit Smirnov was second behind Daehlie in both parts of the event.

On February 27, 1994, the classic 50K was scheduled, the last cross country event and Smirnov's last chance for an Olympic gold. He would be facing all the Norwegian legends as well as several great cross country stars from Italy and Finland. Smirnov had never won a major 50K race, usually tiring badly in the latter stages.

Now in Lillehammer the starters would leave in 30 second intervals. With most of his main opposition starting after him, Smirnov went off at a blistering pace. At every checkpoint he was the fastest of all the skiers. Finally, he approached the 40K checkpoint with ten kilometers left in the race. It was at this point that Smirnov usually tired. But not this day. Smirnov forged on and when he entered the stadium for the last time, it was now evident that at last an Olympic gold medal was his.

There was a little piece of history that took place at the victory podium ceremony. Because of Smirnov's triumph, the national anthem of Kazakhstan was played for the first time at the Olympic Games.

And for Vladimir Smirnov there was an additional honor. For though the anthem being played was that of Kazakhstan, the thousands of flags waving in love and admiration were all Norwegian.

Ulrike Meyfarth

Munich, 1972; Los Angeles, 1984   West Germany

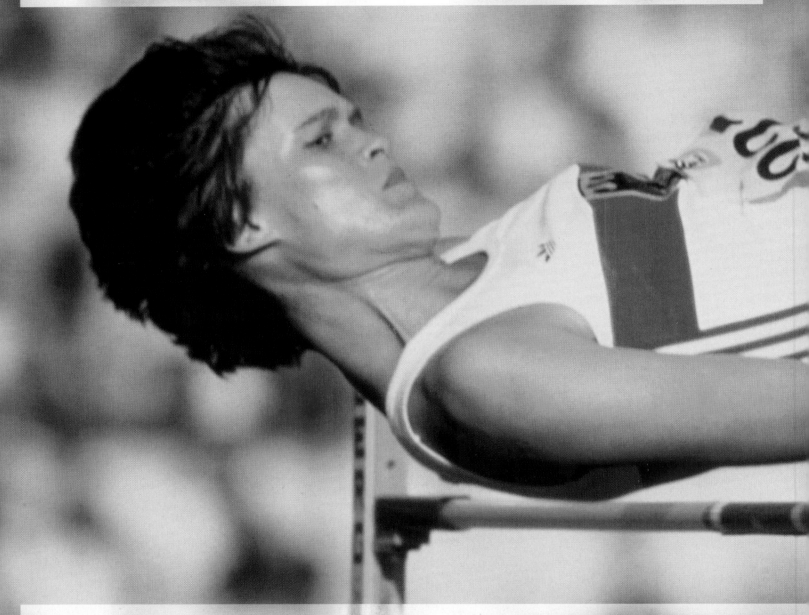

Ulrike Meyfarth, who competed for West Germany before Unification, is one of the most unique performers in Olympic history. She barely made the West German Olympic team for the 1972 Munich Games by coming in third in the high jump trials.

Being so young, she was considered to be in Munich more for experience than for a medal. However, when the high jump competition was over, Meyfarth had won the gold medal and thus became the youngest winner ever in Olympic track and field history. She was sixteen years, 123 days old and because of her youth, Meyfarth seemed destined to have a long career.

Four years later in Montreal, 20-year-old Ulrike Meyfarth failed to make it past the qualifying round. Bad fortune continued to follow Meyfarth when she was unable to compete in the 1980 Moscow Games because of the boycott.

As the 1984 Los Angeles Games approached, she decided to make one more try. "So many things happened to me in the twelve years since I won in Munich," recalled Meyfarth. "At 28 I was older, more mature and pretty certain I could win one of the medals."

Meyfarth's main opposition was expected to come from 31-year-old Sara Simeoni of Italy, who finished sixth at the 1972 Munich Games. But where Meyfarth went into a demise after Munich, Simeoni's career skyrocketed. She won the silver medal in Montreal and the gold in Moscow. Now she would attempt to become the only woman to win the high jump gold medal twice. This, too, was Meyfarth's goal.

As predicted, Meyfarth and Simeoni were the only two left in the battle for the gold medal when the bar reached 6 feet 6 $^3/_4$ inches. Meyfarth had the psychological advantage. She would follow Simeoni. Simeoni went over the height on her first attempt and Meyfarth without hesitation quickly equaled that effort.

The bar was raised three quarters of an inch to 6 feet 7½. . . two inches higher than Simeoni's winning effort four years earlier in Moscow. Simeoni missed on her first attempt. When Meyfarth sailed over on her first try, quickly the pressure went back to Simeoni. The height was too much for the great Italian, whose twelve-year Olympic career would now end with another silver medal. She missed her last two attempts.

For Ulrike Meyfarth there were two more records. She won the title of the oldest woman high jump winner in Olympic history to go along with the youngest title she earned in 1972. Equally prestigious, Meyfarth joined America's four gold medal discus champion Al Oerter as the only track and field athlete to win an individual gold medal twelve years apart in the same event.

Ducky Drake Rome, 1960

The Drake Stadium at UCLA was named after their beloved track and field coach, Elvin "Ducky" Drake. The honor was afforded him while he was still alive.

Drake's pupils have been involved in some of the most dramatic events in sports, but nothing could compare to the 48 hours that confronted Drake during the 1960 Rome Olympic Games. Then he had to witness the titanic struggle in the decathlon between Rafer Johnson of the United States and C.K. Yang of Taiwan. The reason — Ducky Drake was the coach of both men.

While training with Drake at UCLA, Johnson and Yang were like brothers on and off the field. But their friendship would have a two day moratorium in Rome during the decathlon competition.

"They were both my boys," said Drake. "Even though one's an American and one's a Chinese, that couldn't mean anything to me, because I was coaching both of them. And I wanted both of them to have the very best chance to win."

The confrontation was a strange one. At the end of the first five events on the first day, Johnson led Yang by 55 points. But the incredible part of the competition was the fact that Yang did better than Johnson in four of the five events. He was slightly better than Johnson in the 100 meters, long jump, high jump and 400 meter run. But Johnson had an overwhelming victory in the shot put — not only offsetting the slightly better performances of Yang in the four other events, but catapulting Johnson into his 55 point lead after the first day.

The first day performances fulfilled predictions that Yang would be superior in the running and jumping events, but that Johnson would prevail in the strength contests: the shot put, javelin and discus.

Yang immediately went back into the lead in the 110 meter hurdles, the first event of the second day, by soundly defeating Johnson. The win was so big Yang led at the end of six events by 128 points.

But the seventh event was the discus, a throwing event and another crushing victory for Johnson. The swing between the two was 272 points and Johnson now led his UCLA teammate by 144.

Yang came fighting back in the pole vault and cut Johnson's lead by 24 points.

The ninth event was the javelin, and Johnson again expected a big swing. But he gained only an additional 43 points and then led Yang by 67. Now they awaited the tenth and final event — the 1,500 meter run.

"I watched them sitting side by side on the bench. It was cold and they both had blankets around them," remembered Ducky Drake. "Here they are, these two close friends, both afraid to turn and look at each other."

To gain the 68 points to win, Yang would have to defeat Johnson by ten seconds or approximately 50 meters. This was a distinct possibility, since Yang's best 1,500 meter time ever is almost eighteen seconds faster than Johnson's best.

"I knew exactly how the race would be run," said Ducky Drake. "Rafer would stay on C.K.'s shoulder the whole race."

Both men were exhausted during the 1,500 meter ordeal. Every time Yang tried to move away, Johnson moved with him. Finally, at the finish line, Yang was but three meters in front. It was not enough. Yang chipped off but nine points, but Rafer Johnson won the gold medal by 58 points. . .

"If I had my way, both of them should have won gold medals," Drake said sadly. "They were both my boys."

Ducky Drake (far left) coached both C.K. Yang (left) from Taiwan and American Rafer Johnson (right) at UCLA. Though friends off the field, the two were opponents in the 1960 decathlon competition.

145

Abebe Bikila

Rome, 1960; Tokyo, 1964   Ethiopia

There is always a "first" at the Olympic Games, but perhaps the most unlikely first took place at the 1960 Rome Olympics in the marathon.

Then a 28-year-old corporal in Emperor Haille Selassie's Palace Guard, Abebe Bikila, amazed the world by winning the marathon, the most torturous event on the track and field program.

The impassive Bikila, unknown and unheralded, created front page headlines throughout the world not only for becoming the first East African to stand on the top step of the victory podium, but because he ran the entire 26 mile 385 yard distance in his bare feet.

After his victory there were dramatic stories by sportswriters emphasizing the fact that Bikila won despite the fact that his impoverished country did not have the money to supply him with track shoes. The Ethiopian track coach, Negusse Roba, put an end to these stories which he repeatedly called "pure fiction."

"Our whole team was supplied with the best running shoes and Abebe was given several new pairs," said Roba. "A few days before the marathon his regular shoes were wearing thin so a day before the race, he put on a new pair. But they pinched his feet and he complained that they might give him blisters during the race. So he asked if he could run barefoot, for he had practiced many times without shoes."

Four years later at the 1964 Tokyo Games Bikila confirmed Negusse Roba's explanation. At the age of 32 he became the first man in Olympic history to win two successive marathons. He had now won the first and second gold medals ever for an athlete from East Africa.

After Tokyo, Bikila let it be known that he would try for his third gold medal at the 1968 Mexico City Games, when he would be 36 years old.

Suddenly, without warning at the seventeen kilometer mark, Bikila stepped off the roadway and retired from the race. Afterward Negusse Roba told me that Bikila had suffered a bone fracture in his left leg a few weeks earlier, but he wanted to make the attempt. Though in great pain with every step, the injury was never apparent to the spectators. His teammate, Mamo Wolde, inspired by Abebe's courage, surprised everyone by going on to win the race — the third successive marathon victory by an Ethiopian.

After the Mexico City Games, tragedy struck in 1969. Driving his car on a terrible road outside of Addis Ababa, Abebe crashed. Unconscious, he was not found for six hours. His injuries included a broken neck and a severe injury to his spinal cord which left him paralyzed from the waist down.

A few years after his injury I premiered our documentary film on the history of the marathon in Addis Ababa before Emperor Haille Selassie and dignitaries from all of East Africa. Abebe was an important part of the film.

When he arrived at the theater in a wheelchair, he was smiling, an expression I had never seen before, and the thousands in the audience stood as he nodded in appreciation.

I sat next to him during the performance. When he appeared live on the screen, vibrant and in good health as he was in Rome and Tokyo, I turned to see his reaction. A single tear ran down the side of his face and then, unable to control himself, he placed his head in his hand and cried. Abebe passed away in 1973, a national hero.

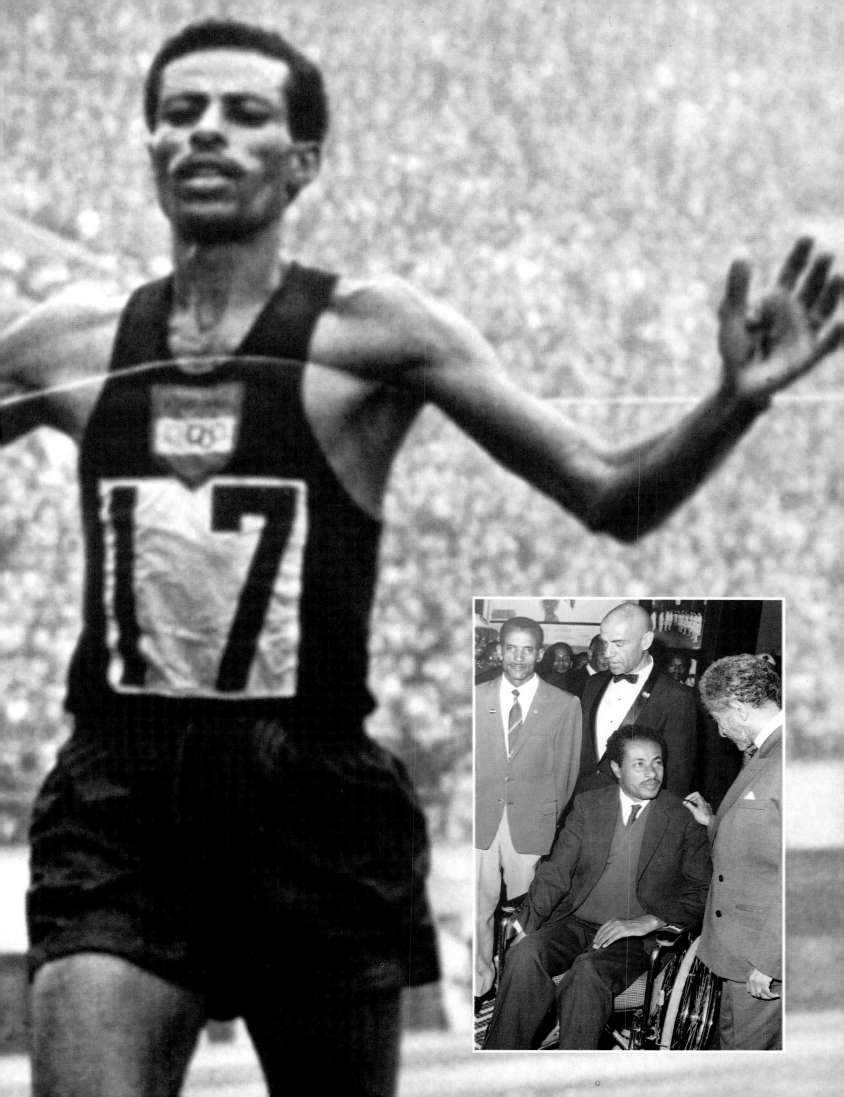

148

Pat McCormick
Helsinki, 1952; Melbourne, 1956   United States

America's all-time Olympic diving queen, Pat McCormick, never gained the international acclaim showered upon Greg Louganis after his victories in the springboard and platform events at the 1984 Los Angeles and 1988 Seoul Olympic Games. But, more than three decades earlier, before Louganis was born, Pat became the first diver to perform the sport's rarest feat — "the double-double."

At the 1948 United States Olympic trials eighteen-year-old Pat Keller missed making the team by less than two points. Patriotism had a lot to do with Pat's desire to try again.

"I remember talking to Vicki Draves, who won both the springboard and platform events at the 1948 London Games," recalled Pat, "and I asked her how she was able to come up with such a magnificent performance. And Vicki said, 'I just looked at my USA uniform and realized I was representing my whole country!' That was my inspiration, too, to try again to become an Olympian."

The year after the London Games Pat married her diving coach, Glenn McCormick. Together they prepared for the 1952 Helsinki Games.

"The routine never changed," said Pat. "One hundred dives a day, six days a week, twelve months a year. You've got to remember, too, there was a lot of walking to the top for the platform diving practice. They didn't have elevators in my day."

In Helsinki Pat was under considerable pressure in the springboard event. Ever since the springboard was introduced for women at the 1920 Antwerp Games, American women had never lost. Pat would try to make it seven straight United States triumphs.

"Helsinki was really fun," smiled Pat. "It was like receiving your first kiss. You never know what to expect.

"After I won I remembered the thrill of standing on the top step of the podium. I still get

goose pimples when I think of the national anthem. I still get tears in my eyes when I think of it."

Pat then went on to win the platform event. Early in 1956, several months before the Melbourne Olympics, Pat McCormick gave birth to her first child, a son.

"At 26 I was the 'old lady' of the team," remembered Pat. "All the other team members were kids. And these kids really looked up to my husband, who was coaching some of them, and I'm saying to myself, 'Hey, what's going on? I'm trying to win again myself and here I am serving breakfast to them in my house.'"

At the 1956 Melbourne Games Pat won the springboard by the largest margin ever. Now she was on the threshold of Olympic history.

"Going into the finals, I was in about third place in the platform," remembered Pat. "With two dives left my teammate Juno Irwin was leading. Then I said to myself, 'You can't go out now after so many years of hard work without a fight.' So I just sat for a moment and made peace with myself. And that did it. I went up there and performed the two best dives of my life." Pat had won her fourth gold medal.

During her career Pat won 77 national titles to go along with her four Olympic gold medals. In recognition of her completing the "double-double" in 1956, Pat won the Sullivan Trophy — awarded annually to the finest amateur athlete of the year, male or female.

Hirofumi Daimatsu

Tokyo, 1964
Japan

Volleyball was introduced as an Olympic sport at the 1964 Tokyo Games. A few years before the Tokyo Olympics were to take place, a women's team called the Kaizuku Amazons was selected to represent Japan in this inaugural event. The team consisted of twelve women who worked for a company called Dai Nippon. The Kaizuku Amazons had an amazing record: They won 137 consecutive games.

Their coach, Hirofumi Daimatsu, an office manager employed by Dai Nippon, was as famous as his team. Preparing for the 1964 Tokyo Games Daimatsu set up a training program that to many was an insult to human dignity. In effect Daimatsu set up a military camp and the team members were conscriptees, there only to obey his commands.

Daimatsu devised a program that defied the imagination. The training sessions were brutal mixtures of mental and physical pain. Scrimmages would consist of non-stop series of dives, rolls and tumbles. Individual sessions were designed to shatter the spirit of the women. Six days a week the women trained. Daimatsu made his team two promises — those who could not survive would be released from the team. But for those who could endure, he promised an Olympic gold medal.

"In Japan I had the reputation of being a devil," said Daimatsu. "However, I believe that when one sets a goal, that one must persevere to achieve such a goal. My goal and the goal of my team was to win an Olympic gold medal."

"There were many times I wanted to quit," said Masae Kasai, the team captain. "It took me a long time to come to the realization that Mr. Daimatsu's principles were not only important for playing volleyball, but they were important principles for life. In particular with talent, dedication and hard work, there is nothing one cannot do."

On October 23, 1964, the Soviet Union and Japan met for the final match of the Olympic championship. Each had won four successive matches and now they would meet in the best three out of five games for the gold medal.

The final was no contest. The Japanese women won the series in three straight games — 15–11, 15–9, 15–13.

On the victory platform as the Japanese national anthem was played in their honor, all twelve of the team members were in tears. By their side was Hirofumi Daimatsu, stoic, and without emotion, standing at attention.

"It was a glorious moment," recalled team captain Masae Kasai. "We all cried for two reasons. We had won the gold medal and had fulfilled our own expectations and that of the Japanese people. Even more, we cried because this would be our last game together, and even though we had been through so much pain and anguish it was worth it. I'm sure we would all do it again."

"I believe that people's true happiness is to be able to look back into their past and feel they worked hard to achieve something and in fact achieved it," said Daimatsu. "They created their own victory. . . They achieved their own goal. As I look back, my happiness was in the fact that I was a part of it."

Kip Keino & Jim Ryun

Mexico City, 1968
Kenya/United States

On Sunday, October 20, 1968, the 1,500 meter run was scheduled at the Mexico City Olympic Games, and the long awaited duel between the world record holder, Jim Ryun of the United States, and Kip Keino of Kenya was about to begin.

Earlier, Keino had to retire from the 10,000 meters with severe stomach cramps. Four days later he was overtaken down the homestretch in the 5,000 meters by Mohamed Gammoudi of Tunisia and had to settle for the silver medal. Now he would make another attempt to become Kenya's second gold medal winner ever, for earlier that week the honor of becoming the first went to his countryman Naftali Temu, who won the 10,000 meters.

Ryun had come through his two 1,500 meter preliminary heats in perfect condition, unaffected by the oppressive Mexico City altitude. In his semi-final, Ryun reinforced the predictions of the experts when he defeated Keino, who by chance was in the same heat.

Kenyan officials recognized they had to devise a plan to neutralize Ryun's strength and speed. They conferred with Ben Jipcho, Keino's teammate, himself a world class runner capable of winning one of the medals in the 1,500 meter final.

"The night before the final the Kenyan officials spoke with me," said Jipcho. "They said, 'Jipcho, you are still young and have a bright future. Kip Keino is getting older and when he quits, it will be your turn. We want you to be the rabbit. We want you to go out very fast, and neutralize the strength of the other runners.'"

The next day, following the pre-race strategy, Jipcho burst out of the pack and went into the lead. Keino and Ryun were content to stay off the punishing pace. There was one major difference in their strategy. Only Keino knew exactly when he would go after his teammate. Ryun did not.

"We knew that Jipcho's pace would physically and psychologically confuse the others," said Charles

Mukora, head of the Kenyan Olympic Committee. "That was our biggest strategy to win the race."

With two laps to go, Keino made his move to overtake his teammate. Ryun decided to wait.

"I was afraid of going too fast," said Ryun. "I was very aware of what altitude could do to an athlete who is used to training at sea-level. I knew if I went too fast I would get into tremendous oxygen debt."

Ryun, in tenth place, bided his time. With a lap and a quarter to go, he began to move up past the runners in front of him, but Keino had built up a tremendous lead and was not slowing down.

"I was passing runners easily, but there were so many in front of me," remembered Ryun. "With 200 meters left, I knew that unless Keino faltered, there was very little chance of catching up with him."

The Kenyan strategy worked to perfection. Keino crossed the finish line ten meters in front of Ryun.

Years later Jipcho was still upset over the Kenyan team strategy.

"It was unfair to people like Jim Ryun," said Jipcho. "It destroyed everybody. Sure, it was good for Kenya. But it was unfair to the other guys."

"If there was a plot, then so be it," said Ryun. "I think it does take away some of the credibility of Kip's victory. In fact Ben Jipcho came over to me later and apologized for having done what he did. He felt that it wasn't fair. I guess it's a matter of what you personally think. My feeling is that the Olympics are supposed to be man against man — not team against man."

At the 1972 Munich Games Kip Keino won the gold medal in the 3,000 meter steeplechase. Ben Jipcho, 'the rabbit' four years earlier, came in second.

Jim Ryun's Olympic career ended in tragedy in the 1972 1,500 meters. Again by the luck of the draw, Ryun and Keino were in the same preliminary heat. With a little more than a lap to go, Ryun was caught on the inside among several runners.

Rather than go outside and easily qualify, Ryun stayed inside, trying to move between runners. He tripped and fell. As the pack moved away, Ryun was sprawled on the track. He got up and caught up with the pack but the distance was too much. Ryun's last Olympic race ended by failing to qualify while Keino went on to win the silver medal in the final behind Finland's Pekka Vasala's thrilling stretch drive victory.

Billy Fiske

Although everyone called him Billy, his full name was William Mead Lindsley Fiske III, who came from a wealthy Chicago banking family. By whatever name, history will record him as America's greatest Olympic and war hero, a man of many "firsts."

Billy's career was right out of an F. Scott Fitzgerald novel. Handsome and wealthy, Fiske was part of the European social scene that congregated in the winter at St. Moritz, Switzerland. Fiske was known as a daredevil with a love for driving the dangerous bobsled. As the 1928 St. Moritz Olympics were but a few months away, Fiske, vacationing with his family at the Olympic site, was selected to drive one of the United States teams entered in the four man event. He was only sixteen years old.

Incredibly, when the competition was over, Billy had driven his team to victory and became the youngest man to ever win a gold medal at the Winter Olympics.

Four years later, 20-year-old Billy Fiske was given the honor of carrying the American flag in the opening day ceremonies of the Lake Placid Olympic Games. He easily won his second gold medal driving the four-man sled.

After his second Olympic victory Fiske's wealth, fame and intelligence made it simple for him to follow in his father's banking success. He joined a prestigious international banking firm, Dillon Read and Co., enabling him to spend half a year in the New York office and the winter in London and making it easier for him to travel to St. Moritz.

There are mixed stories as to why Billy didn't try for his third straight gold medal at the 1936 Games in Garmisch-Partenkirchen, Germany. One was that Billy was angry that, based on his two victories, the United States Olympic Committee should have automatically selected him for the team. Billy felt that he should not have to qualify.

Years later his speedskating teammate Irv Jaffee, himself a double gold medal winner at the 1932 Olympics, recalled vividly that Billy told him that he would not compete in Germany because of his hatred for Adolf Hitler and the Nazi ideology.

Billy remained in Great Britain and in one of the major social events of 1938 married Rose Bingham, the former Countess of Warwick.

His marriage and athletic fame brought him an introduction to Air Chief Marshall, Sir William Elliot, of the Royal Air Force, and when World War II began on September 3, 1939, Billy became one of several Americans to join the Royal Air Force as volunteers. While Hitler was moving through Poland, Fiske was in training as a Hurricane pilot.

In May 1940, when the Nazi blitzkrieg overran France and the Lowlands, the Battle of Britain began. Twenty-nine-year-old Billy Fiske was now a member of the 601 squadron at Tangmere Airfield near London. To counter the almost incessant raids on London, Fiske and his comrades flew day after day, sortie after sortie, often refueling and taking off seven times daily. Over the next few weeks Billy was credited officially with several personal or partial "kills."

On August 16, 1940, one month to the day of his first combat mission, German bombers flew over Tangmere in an attempt to neutralize the base and destroy the British planes on the ground.

Billy took to the skies. In combat with a German bomber, his engine was hit. His plane caught fire, and even though he was badly burned, he was able to land.

He was rushed to the hospital and the prognosis for recovery was good.

"That night several of our squadron visited him in the hospital," recalled the commander of the 601 squadron, Archibald Hope, years later. "They said he was perky as hell, sitting up in bed. The next morning we were stunned. They told us Billy died of shock."

Billy Fiske was given a military funeral in a cemetery outside of London with his squadron comrades as pallbearers. His coffin was draped in British and American flags.

Today a memorial plaque to him remains in St. Paul's Cathedral in London. It reads:

"To Pilot Officer William Mead Lindsley Fiske III. . . an American citizen who died that England might live."

In life Billy Fiske was a man of many firsts. So, too, in death. Billy Fiske was the first American pilot to be killed in World War II.

Billy Fiske, shown at left as driver of the U.S.A. four man bobsled and in inset in British military uniform, was both an enigma and a man of great courage.

Carl Lewis Los Angeles, 1984

 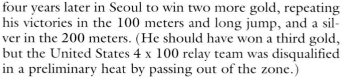

"Jesse Owens was my inspiration," said Carl Lewis after the 1984 Los Angeles Olympics. "Knowing that he had to go through the same things I had to go through at the 1936 Berlin Games inspired me. And then I heard that his wife, Ruth, said that my victories were like watching Jesse, because she didn't have a chance to go see him perform in Berlin."

It is universally known that Carl Lewis duplicated Owens' feat of winning four gold medals in the 100 meters, 200 meters, long jump and as part of the 4 x 100 meter relay team.

"I was so touched that they remembered Jesse at the Los Angeles 1984 opening ceremonies when they let his granddaughter Gina carry the torch into the stadium and hand it over to Rafer Johnson," said Lewis. "I just felt that Jesse was there in spirit."

In three Olympic Games Carl Lewis has established himself as an athletic phenomenon — arguably the greatest performer in the history of the modern Olympics.

After winning four gold medals at the 1984 Los Angeles Games, he came back

four years later in Seoul to win two more gold, repeating his victories in the 100 meters and long jump, and a silver in the 200 meters. (He should have won a third gold, but the United States 4 x 100 relay team was disqualified in a preliminary heat by passing out of the zone.)

At the 1992 Barcelona Olympics at age 31 he won his seventh and eighth gold medals with his third straight long jump victory and then as anchor man on the victorious 4 x 100 relay team. Yet through it all, Lewis' career has been beset with controversy, never reaching the beloved status of his idol, Jesse Owens.

"What bothers me," said Lewis, "is that many people create stories about me out of nowhere. At the 1984 Los Angeles Games people were criticizing me for not taking my last four jumps in the long jump. I had a very good effort on my first jump and thought it was good enough to win. I fouled on the second jump. The weather was getting cold and I had two more events to run, so I made the decision to rise and fall on my first jump. As it happened, it turned out to be the right decision."

Earlier, after winning the 100 meters, there were some criticisms that Lewis had planted a large American flag in the hands of a friend so that he could "showboat" by carrying it around the track in a victory lap. Lewis was upset with these unsubstantiated comments.

"It was spontaneous," said Lewis. "I felt so much pride for the USA, I just wanted to grab something American. I was going around the turn after the race and saw this big American flag in the stands. I beckoned for this guy to come down with the flag and I snatched it from him. His mouth dropped open and he was in shock. So I ran around with the flag and then I returned and handed it back to him. His mouth was still open."

How would Carl Lewis want to be remembered?

"Many people have said, 'You can't do that, Carl. It can't be done. A world class athlete cannot do what you've done. . . to endure so long.' Well, I feel there are no limitations if you broaden your horizons. If you don't succeed you haven't failed, because you can't fail if you've tried your hardest. So I hope I can just be remembered as someone who has inspired people and led them to do things they never thought they could do."

Sonja Henie

St. Mortiz, 1928; Lake Placid, 1932; Garmisch-Partenkirchen, 1936   Norway

Lyudmila and Oleg Protopopov, the 1964 and 1968 gold medal winners from the Soviet Union, are considered by many the greatest pairs skaters in history.

When asked how she first became interested in figure skating, Lyudmila Protopopov replied, "When I was a child I saw Sonja Henie perform in a film called *Sun Valley Serenade*. It was then I knew I wanted to dance on ice."

No athlete has been a greater influence on a sport than Sonja Henie was to women's figure skating. Though she died in 1969, her motion pictures remain as a testament to her greatness both in and out of competition.

After winning Norway's national championship, eleven-year-old Sonja competed in the first Winter Olympic Games in 1924 in Chamonix. She finished last in the competition.

In the next four years, under the guidance of her father, Wilhelm, plans were made for the next Olympics, when she would be fifteen. Wilhelm Henie had grandiose ideas. He would make certain her practice sessions were a combination of her ballet training and athletic ability that would bring to the sport a dramatic program of jumps and spins that at the time were considered revolutionary.

Wilhelm added additional innovations. Sonja would be costumed in short skirts instead of the typical ankle length dresses. The plan worked to perfection. When she was fourteen she won her first world championship in 1927 and the following year in St. Moritz won her first Olympic gold medal.

Sonja continued to win world championships and at the age of nineteen at the 1932 Lake Placid Games easily won her second Olympic gold medal.

"It was most unfortunate for me that I had to be born at the same time she was," remembered Vivi Anne Hulten of Sweden, who finished fifth at the 1932 Games. "It was impossible to beat her. Her dad spent lots of money on her practice sessions and she was always wearing makeup and beautiful clothes. Most of the competitors resented her because in those days amateurs didn't do that."

Winning world championships continued for Sonja between Lake Placid and the 1936 Olympics in Garmisch-

Partenkirchen, Germany. She would win ten world championships in all.

At the 1936 Games, she had to compete before Adolf Hitler and the Nazi hierarchy and once again captivated the judges and audience. Sonja won her third consecutive gold medal, a record that still remains today in women's figure skating.

At the Games there was one incident that would haunt her throughout her lifetime. A photograph was widely circulated showing Sonja giving the Hitler salute — a photograph Nazi propagandists used four years later when Germany occupied Norway during World War II.

After the 1936 Games she turned professional and began a career in motion pictures and as a star of ice shows that made her millions for more than a decade. To this day she is the most commercially successful Olympic champion in history, even though she made her last film almost a half century ago.

George S. Patton Stockholm, 1912

The five event modern pentathlon was introduced on the Olympic program at the 1912 Stockholm Games. The competition had military connotations and in fact was designed specifically for men serving in the armed forces.

The events contested were horseback riding, fencing, pistol shooting, swimming and running and followed a romantic storyline.

The philosophy of this competition was based on a soldier being ordered to deliver a message on horseback. When he was confronted by the enemy, he was forced to dismount and "duel" with a sword in order to escape. Continuing his mission, he "shot" his way out of danger. Then the messenger might have to "swim" across a river and "run" almost three miles before he finally delivered the message.

At the 1912 Games Swedish officers won the gold, silver and bronze medals. The Swedes were so strong, they finished in the top six out of seven positions.

The only "outsider" who gave them any competition was 26-year-old United States Army Lieutenant George S. Patton. Patton went on to become one of the most brilliant and controversial generals of World War II, with the nickname "Blood and Guts."

George S. Patton (right) on his way to fourth place in the fencing event in the pentathlon of the 1912 Games. Some bad luck in the shooting event may have cost Patton the gold medal. In background: The field in Stockholm where the pentathlon was contested.

United States

Brilliance and controversy for Patton was much in evidence at the Olympic Games. Before the competition began it was predicted that Patton had a good chance of winning the gold medal. He was proficient in all five events.

Thirty-two contestants entered and the consistent Patton was vying with the leaders in four of the five events. He finished seventh in swimming, fourth in fencing, sixth in riding and third in running. His combined total placed him in a position to win the gold medal.

But a major controversy arose in pistol shooting — Patton's first event and a skill he practiced with uncanny preci-

sion — when officials claimed that one of his attempts completely missed the target.

Patton and American officials argued that the one shot they claimed had missed in reality had passed through the hole of a previous shot — the reason for no mark on the target. The protest was denied. Patton finished in 21st place in pistol shooting. When added to his other four event total Patton overall was in fifth place.

During World War II General Patton became internationally known for wearing pearl handled pistols. Romantic history writers have claimed through the years that Patton wore the pistols to remind him in battle "that nothing is certain."

Eddie Eagan

Antwerp, 1920; Lake Placid, 1932   United States

Eddie Eagan's academic credentials were impeccable — a Yale University degree, a Harvard Law School graduate and a Rhodes Scholar.

When the Olympic Games were renewed in Antwerp in 1920 after World War I canceled the 1916 Games, Eagan was captain of the Yale boxing team. After making the United States Olympic team, Eagan went on to win the light-heavyweight Olympic boxing gold medal. Afterward he became amateur champion in both Great Britain and the United States.

"He was afraid of nothing," said his wife, Peggy. "He was really a world champion. He and a friend took a trip around the world and in every country Eddie challenged the amateur champion and finished the tour undefeated. So when you talk about undefeated champions, my husband was one of them."

With his Olympic days apparently over, Eagan started a successful law practice.

As the 1932 Winter Olympic Games approached, Eagan had a momentous meeting with Jay O'Brien, the chairman of the United States bobsled selection committee. "Jay O'Brien was a close friend of ours," remembered Peggy Eagan. "One night Eddie came back from dinner with Jay and said, 'Guess what. I'm on the United States bobsled team.' I was shocked because Eddie had never been on a bobsled before."

Eagan was now a member of one of the two United States sleds entered in the 1932 Lake Placid Games. The group was one of the strangest foursomes ever assembled for a bobsled event.

The driver was 20-year-old Billy Fiske, a socialite daredevil who four years earlier at the age of sixteen drove his sled to the four-man victory at the St. Moritz Olympics. Eddie Eagan would be in the number two spot followed by Clifford Gray, a successful songwriter. The brakeman was Jay O'Brien, the U.S. bobsled committee chairman.

"Eddie was absolutely fearless. He would try everything just for the thrill of it," said Peggy Eagan. "After a few practice sessions they performed like they had been together for years."

In the first three of the four run event Eagan's team had an insurmountable lead. They coasted in the fourth run, making certain to remain on the course, and their combined four run total time gave them the victory by more than two seconds.

For Billy Fiske and Clifford Gray, it was their second successive Olympic bobsled victory. For Eddie Eagan, it was his second gold medal garnered twelve years after his boxing victory. Even more for Eddie Eagan, a singular honor still remains today. He is the only athlete, male or female, to have won gold medals at both the Winter and Summer Olympics.

Eddie Eagan is the only individual to have won a gold medal in both the Summer and Winter Games: as light heavyweight champion in 1920 (right) and as member of the U.S.A.'s gold medal winning four man bobsled team in 1932 (below, second from front).

Johann Olav Koss

Lillehammer, 1994

Norway

On Sunday afternoon, February 20, 1994, 12,000 cheering spectators packed the Viking Ship Arena for the men's 10,000 meters, the last event on the men's speed skating program at the Lillehammer Olympics.

Banners inscribed with the words "Koss is Boss" bedecked the arena as the crowd sang the familiar "Victory is Ours" time and time again. Finally Johann Olav Koss appeared on the ice for the fifth pairing of the 10,000 meter final. When his name was announced many thousands of Norwegian flags waved in salute and the crowd roared. In the past week their beloved hero had endeared himself not only to Norwegians, but to the entire world.

Seven days earlier 25-year-old Johann Olav Koss won the 5,000 meters against the best in the world, creating a world record. Until his victory, his physical condition was suspect. It had been reported that Koss, a medical student, was suffering from a knee injury.

"I tried to keep it a secret within the team members," said Koss, "but it leaked out. The press made it a bigger thing than it was. I was in excellent shape when the Games began."

Three days after his 5,000 meter win, Koss was at the starting line for the 1,500 meters. He was not one of the favorites for the gold medal, being ranked only sixth in the world cup standings. The favorites were two skaters from Holland, Rintje Ritsma, the 1,500 meter world record holder, and his countryman Falko Zandstra.

Koss skated in the second pair, giving an advantage to the two Dutch skaters who were in later pairings and would know the time they had to beat. Koss, however, was magnificent. He broke Ritsma's world record and went into first place.

Zandstra skated a speedy fifth race and was leading Koss at the various checkpoints. But he had gone too fast too early and was slowing down in his last lap. At the finish he was more than a second behind Koss's world record time.

Ritsma, was faster than Koss at the early checkpoints, but he also pushed himself too far. On the final lap he knew it was all over. At the finish he trailed Koss by more than a half second. Koss had won his second gold medal in world record time followed by the two Dutch superstars, Ritsma and Zandstra in second and third place.

After his victory Koss held a press conference. He had decided to donate his $30,000 prize money to Olympic Aid, a Norwegian charity to assist children in war-torn areas such as Sarajevo, site of the 1984 Winter Olympics.

"I saw all those terrible pictures of the people of Sarajevo, particularly the children. I figured how lucky I have been," said Koss, "and I thought it right that I should share it with those who really need it."

Four days after his 1,500 meter victory, Koss stepped to the starting line for the 10,000 meters. He had held the world record in this event for more than three years.

"I decided to race the 10,000 as if it was the 5,000," Koss recalled. "I never skated like that before but I wanted to try it."

Koss was spectacular. He quickly went out to a big lead over his partner Frank Dittrich of Germany. "It was crazy. The ice was so fast," said Koss afterward. "I was getting farther and farther ahead of Frank Dittrich and soon I was passing him, one lap ahead. That is impossible to believe. I keep saying to myself, 'Wow, this is something!' I was tired, but the crowd urged me on. It was unbelievable."

When he crossed the finish line Koss looked to the scoreboard, almost in disbelief. Then he raised his arms skyward in a victory salute. He had broken his own world record by an amazing thirteen seconds.

Johann Olav Koss stood on the victory platform for the third time and in doing so created his third world record.

Johann Olav Koss had become a living example of the words that have sent Olympians into the arena for decades:

"Never look to the ground for your next step. Greatness belongs to those who look to the horizon."

Ágnes Keleti

Helsinki, 1952; Melbourne, 1956   Hungary

In 1939 Ágnes Keleti was one of Hungary's gymnastic hopefuls to win a medal at the 1940 Olympics, which were canceled because of World War II. Though it was a severe setback for Ágnes, it could not compare to what would happen to her during the war. In 1940 the Hungarian gymnastic clubs expelled non-Aryan members. Ágnes Keleti was Jewish.

When Nazi Germany moved their forces into Hungary in 1941, the Keleti family went into hiding. Though her sister and mother were saved by the inter-

vention of Raoul Wallenberg, her father was sent to Auschwitz, where he died in a gas chamber.

Ágnes, on her own, was able to purchase false identity papers from a Christian girl and she spent the war working as a maid for a German general stationed in Budapest. During this time she was able to make contact with her mother and sister and every week would smuggle food for them from the table of the general she worked for.

With peace in 1945, 24-year-old Ágnes, who had little time to train during the war, started a comeback. She had an Olympic dream. When it appeared that the Olympic Games would be renewed in London in 1948, Ágnes, now 27, went into serious training. Amazingly, at this late age, she made the team.

Three days before the competition was to begin in London, tragedy again struck Ágnes Keleti. During one of her final training sessions she tore a ligament in her ankle and could not compete. She spent the time in London as a spectator on crutches.

Ágnes would not quit. When the 1952 Helsinki Olympic Games came around, Ágnes was 31. She again made the Hungarian team and then stunned the world by winning an Olympic gold medal in the floor exercise and a silver and two bronze in other disciplines.

Ágnes had finally fulfilled her dream and for all intents and purposes her career was over. However, she continued to train and teach young Hungarian gymnasts for future Olympic Games.

As 1956 came around, the freedom movement from the Communist regime was rising in Hungary. Ágnes became a part of it. She had lived through the Nazi occupation and one way or another, she would not become part of a suppressed society again.

As the Soviets were threatening the Hungarian uprisings, Ágnes at age 35 decided to try for the Olympic team again. She realized this was one way of getting out of the country. Astoundingly, she made the team for the third time.

As the Soviets were putting down the uprisings with tanks and shells, Ágnes was in Melbourne accomplishing one of the great unknown feats in Olympic history. She won four gymnastic gold medals — repeating her gold medal victory in the floor exercise and adding additional gold in the balance beam, asymmetrical bars and as part of the Hungarian portable apparatus team, an event no longer contested. Ágnes is still in the record book as the oldest gymnast gold medal winner in Olympic history.

When the Hungarian revolt was suppressed by the Soviets, Ágnes decided to make a new life. She accepted an invitation to become a citizen of Israel, where she found her true happiness. She married an Israel and had two children when she was 42 and 44 years old. Her reply when people question the late age of the births: "They didn't believe I could win a gold medal when I was 35 and I won four. My children were just two more gold medals."

Daley Thompson

Los Angeles, 1984

Great Britain

On the afternoon of August 9, 1984, defending Olympic decathlon champion Daley Thompson from Great Britain was in the worst crisis of his career... Jurgen Hingsen, his great rival from West Germany, was just 108 points behind him after six events in the ten event decathlon. The winner would earn the title of "the world's greatest all-around athlete."

The decathlon is a two day competition, five events the first day and five the second — a combination of the individual athlete's prowess in running, jumping and throwing.

After the first day's events, the 100 meters, long jump, shot put, high jump and 400 meters, Thompson led Hingsen by 114 points. The second day would include the 110 meter hurdles, discus, pole vault and javelin and end with the grueling 1,500 meter run.

There is a scoring table for each event — the better the performance, the higher the score. The highest combined score at the conclusion of the ten events is the winner.

In the first event of the second day, the 110 meter hurdles, Hingsen gained back six points, running the distance slightly faster than Thompson, and now trailed by 108 points.

The discus was the seventh event and each competitor would have three throws. Hingsen immediately let Thompson know the challenge was on.

On his second attempt, Hingsen hurled the discus 166 feet 9 inches, his greatest throw ever and a decathlon Olympic record.

Thompson failed miserably on his first two attempts. His best effort was more than 30 feet shorter than Hingsen's.

With each man having one throw left, an incredible point swing in favor of Hingsen was a distinct possibility.

If neither athlete improved on his final attempt, the six foot seven inch West German champion would take the lead by 68 points.

Hingsen could not improve on his final throw, but he walked over to me smiling broadly.

"Bud, now the competition begins," he said to me.

Thompson stepped into the discus ring and stood motionless for several seconds as if in a trance. Then he began his twirling motion that would generate the power for his throw.

"This was my test. . . this was my moment," Thompson recalled. "Everything at the end of the day has got to be a test. Everything that has gone before has no meaning. This was the moment to step to the edge of the cliff and not be afraid to look down. . . This was my moment."

When Thompson's throw landed, the crowd roared. Thompson wiggled his hips as if he were a belly dancer, then jumped in the air, raising his arms high overhead.

Thompson knew he had thrown his best distance ever, even though it was fourteen feet less than Hingsen's best effort. Though he lost some of his lead points, he was still in first place by 32 points.

Hingsen was crushed. His body language as he walked from the discus area was that of a defeated athlete — one whose chance had come and gone.

An exuberant Thompson came over to me, smiling and triumphant, even though the pole vault, javelin and 1,500 meters still were to be contested.

"What did Hingsen say to you after his second throw?" Thompson asked me.

"Now the competition begins," I told Daley.

"Go over and tell him he's right," laughed Daley. "The competition has just started for second place."

Thompson was right. He demolished Hingsen in the pole vault and javelin, then leisurely moved through the 1,500 meters, only having to finish the race to insure his victory.

Daley Thompson had won his second straight decathlon gold medal, defeating Hingsen by 124 points.

Tony Sailer

Cortina d'Ampezzo, 1956   Austria

Jean-Claude Killy's victories in all three alpine skiing events at the 1968 Grenoble Olympics are known to millions throughout the world. It was particularly significant since Killy's feat took place in France, his homeland.

Killy's victories have all but obscured an even greater individual performance that took place twelve years earlier at the 1956 Cortina d'Ampezzo Games. There Austria's Tony Sailer amazed the world by becoming the first man not only to sweep all three alpine events, but to sweep them in such an overwhelming fashion that in effect his opponents were skiing for the silver and bronze medals. The gold was exclusively the property of Tony Sailer.

Sailer's first event was the giant slalom, and when the competition was finished, Sailer had won the gold by an amazing 6.2 seconds. "I couldn't believe it," says Sailer. "I told them it was impossible. That they should check their watches. I knew that I was skiing fast. But winning by more than six seconds. That is impossible."

Two days later Sailer was in the slalom — two runs down a twisting course of gates and sharp turns. "I was the fastest in both runs and again my margin of victory was difficult to believe," said Sailer. "I had won by *Four* full seconds."

Next came the treacherous downhill, on a day that was highlighted by strong winds. The course was so dangerous that more than one third of the 75 men entered failed to make it to the finish line.

"A few minutes before I started my run I noticed that one of my ski bindings had broken and I had to borrow a binding from an old friend who was a coach of the Italian team," recalled Sailer. "My coach was very nervous and he kept banging me on the shoulder to make sure I was ready. He kept saying, 'Don't be nervous, you'll make it.' That was very strange because I wasn't at all nervous. He was nervous. And I kept thinking, if he puts his hand on my shoulder one more time I'm going to hit him."

Sailer's downhill run was as impeccable as his two previous gold medal victories. Remarkably, he again won by an overwhelming margin — 3½ seconds.

Sailer returned to Austria a national hero and was besieged with offers from record album promoters and motion picture producers. His success in the entertainment world fell far short of what many believe to be the greatest individual performance in Winter Olympic history.

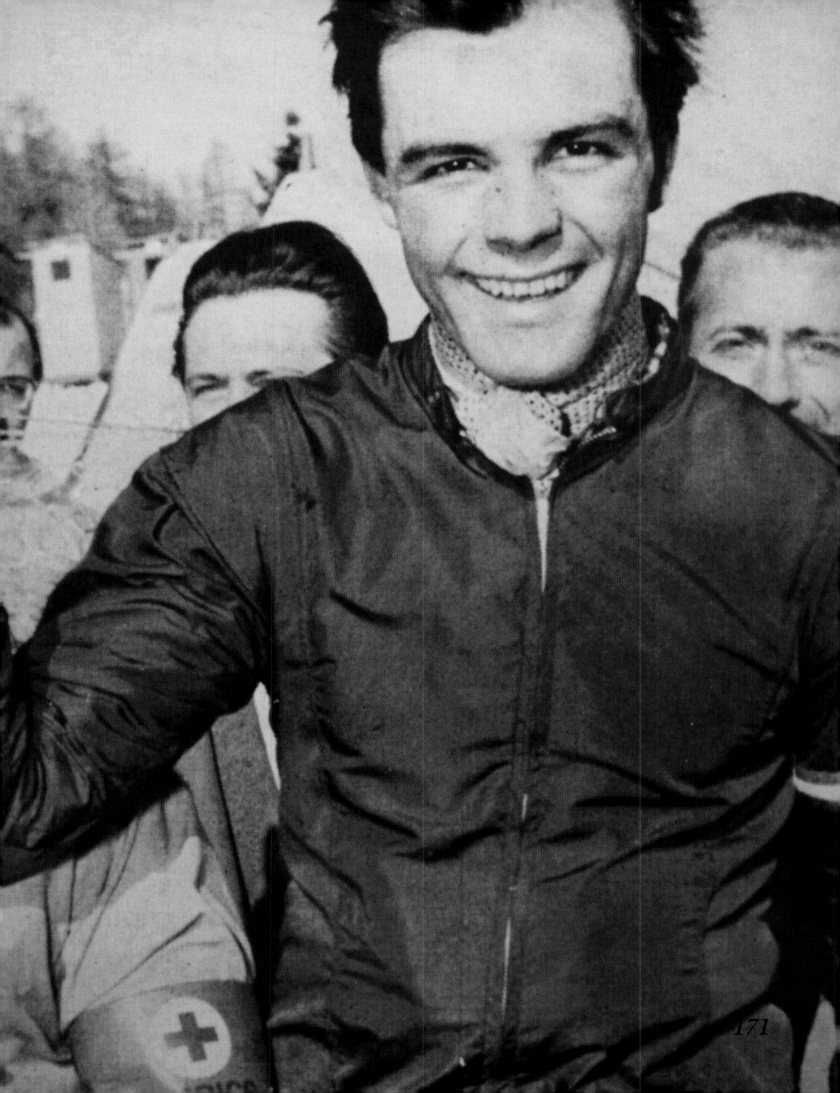

John Devitt & Lance Larson

The greatest controversy in the history of Olympic swimming took place in the 100 meter freestyle at the 1960 Rome Olympics — the duel between John Devitt of Australia and Lance Larson of the United States.

With 20 meters left in the race, Devitt was inches ahead of Larson, but the American was gaining with each stroke as they neared the wall for the finish.

As soon as Larson touched the wall underwater, he immediately looked for his time on the scoreboard. Devitt touched above the water, which was easier for the judges to see. This was the era before electric timing took precedent over the possibility of human judging error.

The six judges at the finish assigned to decide first and second place were evenly divided. Three picked Larson and three picked Devitt.

The chief judge, seated five meters from the finish and with no vote, illegally broke the tie and ruled that Devitt was the winner.

However, there were three "unofficial" timers assigned to each lane. All three of Devitt's times clocked him in 55.2. The timers in Larson's lane caused an incredible dilemma. One timer caught Larson in 55 seconds flat and the other two timed the American in 55.1. All three timers had Larson finishing in a faster time than the Australian.

United States officials protested, but to no avail. The decision stood. Devitt remained the winner with Larson the silver medalist. The final embarrassment came later. Since it's impossible for the second place finisher to have a time faster than the winner, Larson's time was changed to that of Devitt — both now are recorded in the record book with the time 55.2.

Wilma Rudolph

Rome, 1960

United States

There is no Olympic champion that had greater hardships to overcome than Wilma Rudolph. As a child, she was unable to walk without a brace on her left leg because of illnesses that included double pneumonia and scarlet fever. Wilma not only shed the brace when she was eleven, but nine years later she went on to win three gold medals at the 1960 Rome Olympics and perhaps became the most beloved female athlete the United States ever produced.

"Every Saturday when I was a kid my mom would take me on a bus from our home in Clarksville, Tennessee, to a Nashville hospital 60 miles away for treatment on my leg," wrote Wilma in her autobiography. "Then during the week my brothers and sisters would take turns massaging my leg. If it wasn't for my family, I probably would never have been able to walk properly, no less run."

Wilma became a basketball star in high school and her speed on the court was spotted by Ed Temple, coach of the famed Tennessee State "Tigerbelles" track team.

"Coach Temple was refereeing one of our basketball games when I was fifteen," Wilma recalled. "He invited me to attend his summer camp. My dad didn't want me to leave home. I had been so sheltered he was afraid of me going into the outside world. That I was too young. He told Coach Temple, 'My baby has had enough troubles.'"

Her father finally relented and the following year Wilma was good enough at age sixteen to make the Olympic team for the 1956 Melbourne Games.

Wilma was eliminated in the first round of the 200 meters but ran the third leg on the 4 x 100 relay team that won the bronze medal. The "trouble" her father feared became a reality two years before the 1960 Rome Olympics when Wilma gave birth to a baby girl fathered by her boyfriend, Robert Eldridge, whom she later married.

Her father did not want her to go to Rome. Rather, he was adamant that she stay home and be a good mother to her child.

But Wilma's mother, Blanche, and Coach Ed Temple finally prevailed. It was now predicted that Wilma would become the star of the Games.

Trouble followed her to Rome. The day before she was to compete in her qualifying heat of the 100 meters, the first of her three events, she tripped over a water main after a practice session and severely sprained her ankle. For a time it was uncertain whether she would make it to the starting line. Fortunately the swelling subsided that night, but she had to tape her ankle throughout the competition.

After winning the 100 meters, foreign newspapers headlined her as "The Black Gazelle." She followed this victory with another win in the 200 meters and then ran the anchor leg on the victorious 4 x 100 relay team. She now was the darling of the Games and holder of the title of "the fastest woman in the world."

But the real measure of what endeared Wilma to millions was her reply to the often asked question, "What was the victory that was most important to you?"

"Oh, without question it was the relay," she always replied. "For then I could stand on the podium with my Tigerbelle teammates whom I love. . . and we could celebrate together."

Maurilio De Zolt

Lillehammer, 1994   Italy

On Tuesday, February 22, 1994, thousands of Norwegians gathered at the cross country course in Lillehammer to witness the men's 4 x 10 kilometer relay.

The race had particular significance to Norwegians because it was a team event — four men per team from fourteen countries each skiing ten kilometers. It is one of the few events not decided by time. With the teams starting side by side, the winner was the first to cross the finish line.

Leading to this race, the Norwegian superstars had been overwhelming. In Albertville two years earlier the Norwegians won all five events including the relay. Here in Lillehammer they won the first three men's events contested — eight successive victories in two Olympics. Only Italy and Finland were given a chance of upsetting the Norwegians in the relay.

The first leg was perhaps the most critical part of the race, especially for the Italian team. Their chances for staying in contention were dependent on the "old man," 43-year-old Maurilio De Zolt.

De Zolt started his Olympic career fourteen years earlier at the 1980 Lake Placid Games when he was 29, but he won no medals. Amazingly, however, he won silver medals in the taxing 50 kilometer races in Calgary and Albertville when he was 37 and 41 years old.

"People wonder how I lasted so long. Well, I believe in special foods and drink — particularly pasta and a lot of good red wine," laughed De Zolt. "I will not tell you how many glasses I drink, for if I told you I would get in a lot of trouble."

De Zolt's task was a formidable one. He must ski against the great Sture Sivertsen of Norway, who won the 10K world championship one year earlier.

"The 10K is not my favorite race. Sivertsen not only won the individual 10K world championship, he also skied the first leg against me when the Norwegians won the world relay title. He beat me by more than one minute and made their victory easy," recalled De Zolt. "I must do better today or the result will be the same."

When the race got under way it immediately became obvious that it would be a duel among three countries — Norway, Finland and Italy. They left the rest of the field behind.

At the first passoff the crowd was amazed, not that Norway and Finland were inches apart for the lead, but that 43-year-old Maurilio De Zolt was in third place, only ten seconds behind.

De Zolt's performance gave inspiration to the Italian team. For the rest of the race the three teams took turns leading the race — always within a few feet of each other.

Finally on the last leg, Norway's great champion, Bjorn Daehlie, was pitted against Italy's Silvio Fauner. The fact that Daehlie had won five gold medals in Albertville and Lillehammer had no meaning. This race was head to head and Fauner was an outstanding sprinter. With 100 meters left Fauner was a few feet ahead. Daehlie tried desperately to pass him but could not. Italy had broken Norway's gold medal streak at eight and were Olympic champions.

Though Fauner was first across the finish line, he knew where the race was won. After the victory ceremony Fauner said, "Through the years people have asked me who is my hero, who is my inspiration. The answer is simple, for it is the same person. . . his name is Maurilio De Zolt."

On Sunday evening, September 25, 1988, 10,000 spectators filled the Seoul Olympic natatorium for the final events of the seven day swimming competition. It would be a historic evening for three magnificent champions.

In the men's 4 x 100 meter medley relay, Matt Biondi of the United States swam the third leg, the butterfly, as the American foursome set a world record. For Biondi it was the climax of an astounding week. . . In seven events he won five gold, one silver and one bronze medal. Two gold were in individual events, the 50 and 100 meter freestyle, and three were as a member of victorious American relay teams.

Also on this night, 22-year-old Kristin Otto of East Germany completed the greatest performance ever turned in by a female swimmer. After she won the 50 meter freestyle, she stood on the top step of the victory podium for the sixth time. . . the winner of four individual and two relay gold medals. Incredibly, her four individual medals were won with three different strokes. She won the 50 and 100 meter freestyle, the 100 meter butterfly and the 100 meter backstroke.

But if Biondi and Otto were the greatest gold medal winners in Seoul, it remained for the men's 1,500 meter freestyle to provide the most poignant climax to the week:

the final Olympic appearance of Vladimir Salnikov of the Soviet Union. Salnikov is a swimming legend, but at age 28 was considered past his prime. From 1978 to 1986 he was virtually unbeatable in the 400, 800 and 1500 meter freestyle distances.

At the 1980 Moscow Games, which many western countries boycotted, Salnikov won three gold medals. His 1,500 meter victory created history — he became the first man to swim the distance under fifteen minutes — a barrier in swimming that was equal to Roger Bannister breaking the four minute mile. He also won the 400 meters and was part of the victorious Soviet relay team. As a world record holder of the 800 meters, he probably would have won this event, but it was not on the Olympic program.

For almost ten years, 1977 to 1986, Salnikov was unbeaten in the 1,500 meters, racking up 61 consecutive victories. But two years before the Seoul Games, he came in fourth in the 1,500 world championships and failed to qualify for the European championship 1,500 meter final.

Totally depressed, Salnikov sought out a new coach, his wife, Marina. "We worked well together," said Salnikov. "My friends told me I should retire but Marina always cheered me up. She would always say, 'You can do it.'"

Eight men lined up for the final of the 1,500 meter

freestyle, the last event on the Seoul Olympic swimming program. Salnikov qualified in the second fastest time behind that of Matt Cetlinski of the United States.

Cetlinski took the lead for the first 700 meters but just before the halfway point, Salnikov went past him. However, there were two uncertain factors: Salnikov's age and condition. He was 28 years old and the day before he swam a grueling qualifying race.

But Salnikov did not falter. He broke Cetlinski's will to stay with him. Salnikov continued but with 100 meters left he was exhausted.

"I told myself there is no 1500 meters today. . . all I can go is 1,400 meters," remembered Salnikov. "But then, when I touched the wall with 100 meters left, I said to myself, 'OK. . . I change my mind. . . I will go another 100 meters.'"

During the last 50 meters, the crowd was on its feet cheering, "Vladimir. . . Vladimir. . ." and when the victory was his, the cheers reverberated throughout the stadium.

When the awards ceremony was completed and the Soviet national anthem had been played in his honor, Salnikov announced his retirement.

"When someone reaches the top, one feels that he has done all he set out to do," said Salnikov. "I can say yes, I did everything but that does not mean it is over. Now I must find another mountain to climb."

The Last Man in the Marathon

Mexico City, 1968

Tanzania

The marathon run at the 1968 Mexico City Olympics was filled with drama. The legendary Abebe Bikila, who had won the previous two marathons in Rome and Tokyo, was attempting to make it three successive victories. It would add a new dimension to a record he already held, for Bikila at that time was the only marathon runner to ever win that event twice.

Bikila looked strong and was among the leaders at seventeen kilometers, more than one third into the race. . . . Then suddenly and inexplicably, except to his coach, Negusse Roba, he stepped off the roadway and retired from the race. Roba later told a stunned press conference audience that Bikila had been suffering from a bone fracture in his left leg for several weeks.

Bikila's teammate, Mamo Wolde, knew of the injury and when Bikila left the race, Wolde ran as if he was Bikila's mirror image and was able to give Ethiopia its third successive marathon victory, which he later dedicated to his idol, Abebe.

But the drama of this particular marathon would not end when Wolde crossed the finish line. A little more than an hour later with just a few thousand spectators left in the stands, whistles, motorcycle sounds and flashing red and green lights gave a macabre effect to the cold, dark Mexico City evening. . . The word was passed to the press box and filtered to the few thousand faithful spectators who remained in the stadium.

"It's the last runner in the marathon," said one reporter as he stopped typing his story to watch the event developing in front of him.

Into the stadium came John Stephen Akhwari of Tanzania. His leg was bloody and bandaged. Wincing with pain at every step, he pressed on and the thousands, a few minutes before in silence, began a slow, steady clapping.

Akhwari made his painful way around the track and the cheering grew louder. The trek around the track seemed interminable. But finally he hobbled across the finish and the crowd roared as if he had been the winner.

In the press box one columnist was writing this lead to his story.

"Today we have seen a young African runner who symbolizes the finest in the human spirit. . . a performance that gives true meaning to sport. . . a performance that lifts sport out of the category of grown men playing at games. . . a performance that gives meaning to the word courage. . . all honor to John Stephen Akhwari of Tanzania."

Afterward Akhwari was asked why he endured the pain and why, since there was no chance of winning, he did not retire from the race. Akwari appeared perplexed at the question. Then he simply said, "I don't think you understand. My country did not send me to Mexico City to start the race. They sent me to finish the race."

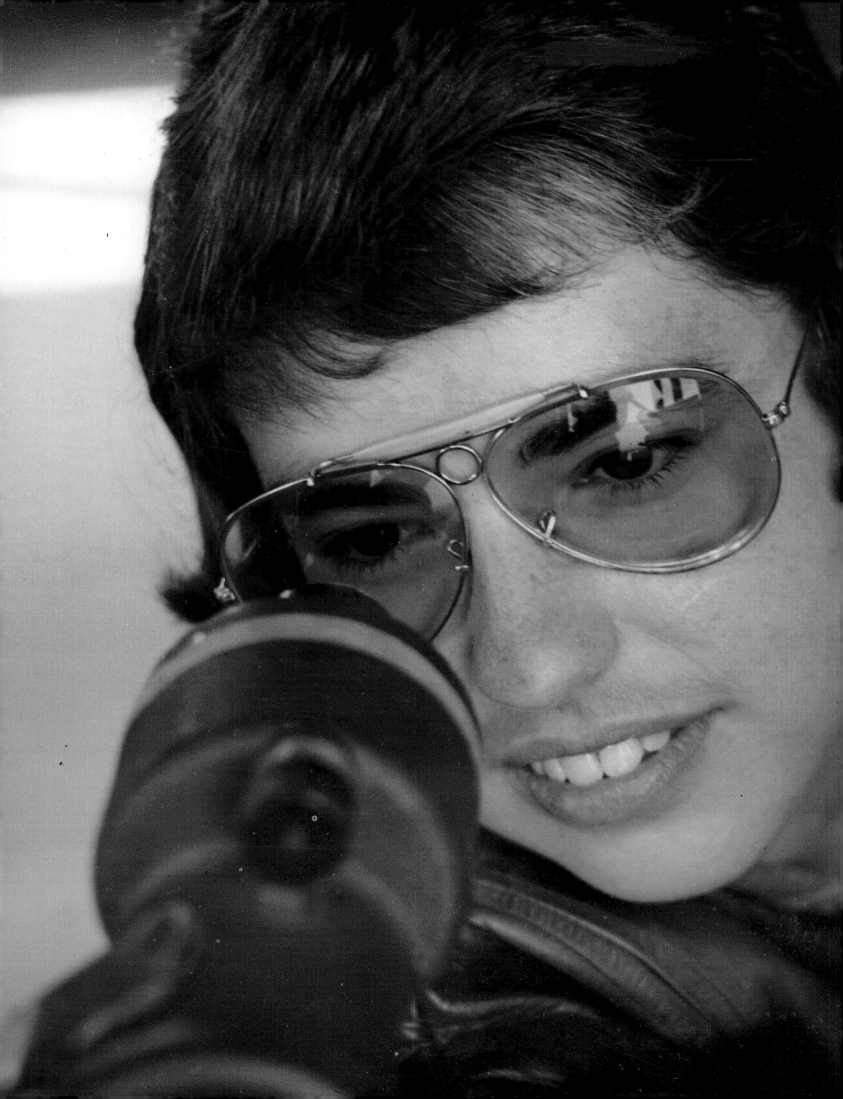

Margaret Murdock

The small-bore rifle competition at the 1976 Montreal Olympics was perhaps the least known dramatic final of the Games. The event consists of shooting at targets from three positions: prone, standing and kneeling. The favorite in the competition was Lanny Bassham of the United States, who won the silver medal four years before in Munich.

Bassham's main opposition was expected to come from his teammate, 33-year-old Margaret Murdock, the mother of a small child and in her last year of study at nursing school.

Margaret Murdock is considered one of the great champions in United States history — one of the few women able to compete on an equal basis with the male champions of her sport. She's won seven individual world championships, fourteen world team championships and five Pan-American gold medals and has held numerous individual and team world records. She is the only woman ever to be ranked in the world's top ten greatest shooters list by the International Shooting Union.

Murdock had already added another "first" to her long list of accomplishments by becoming the first female member of a United States Olympic Shooting Team. Now in Montreal she would be battling to become the first woman to win a medal in an Olympic shooting competition.

The competition was close throughout. When the last rounds were fired, the crowd roared its approval. Murdock's name stood first on the scoreboard with 1,162 points, one more than her countryman Lanny Bassham.

As the Americans prepared for the victory ceremony, the officials were having an animated discussion. Finally it was announced that due to a clerical error one of the judges had written a "nine" on Bassham's score when it should have been a "ten." Now both Murdock and Bassham were in a flatfooted tie — each with 1,162 points. Murdock was thrilled for her teammate, for now each would be awarded a gold medal.

But the officials called for another meeting. Further investigation of the Federation rules determined there were measures to break ties. Bassham's score included three 100's to two for Murdock. Bassham was awarded the gold medal and Murdock the silver.

The final decision did not stand well with Bassham as he stood on the top step of the victory platform. As the "Star Spangled Banner" was about to be played, he reached down and clasped Murdock's hand, beckoning her to join him on the top step of the podium. Together they shared the highest step.

"I wanted to show that I felt her performance equaled mine," said Bassham afterward. "There was no way she deserved to stand lower while the anthem was played."

Dan Jansen

Lillehammer, 1994   United States 🇺🇸

When the final results of the men's 500 meter speed skating event at the 1984 Sarajevo Olympics were announced, eighteen-year-old Dan Jansen of the United States was happy. He had finished in fourth place, only thirty-six-hundredths of a second behind the gold medal winner.

"I was so thrilled just to be in the Olympics," said Jansen. "When I got to Sarajevo I thought I had a chance to finish in the top ten. It was beyond my hopes to finish fourth. Then when I got home, the reaction was different. Some of the press had written, 'Fourth place. . . too bad. . . no medal.' And that's when you first realize what the press does for medals in this country."

Four years later in Calgary, Jansen was one of the favorites in both the 500 and 1,000 meters. Yet he had to face this challenge with the knowledge that his beloved sister Jane was dying of leukemia.

"On the morning of the 500 meter race Mom called and told me that Jane probably wouldn't make it through the day," Jansen recalled. "I talked to Jane one last time and told her I was going to win for her. She couldn't talk, but Mom told me she was nodding and understood what I was saying."

Jansen skated in the second pair and started off swiftly. But less than 100 meters later he was sprawling on the ice after a bad fall.

Four days later in the 1,000 meters, tragedy again struck. With one lap to go and with the fastest time of all the previous skaters, Jansen again fell. In the two races he was expected to medal, he failed to finish.

Four years later at the 1992 Albertville Games, again one of the favorites in both events, Jansen was unable to fulfill the pre-Olympic predictions. He finished fourth in the 500 meters and a disastrous 26th in the 1,000 meters.

With the change of the Winter Olympic cycle, Jansen would make one more try two years later at the 1994 Lillehammer Games.

Leading to Lillehammer, his credentials were now monumental. He was the world record holder in the 500 meters and the only skater ever to go the distance under 36 seconds — a feat comparable to Roger Bannister running the mile under four minutes in track.

"I was sure I would win the 500 meters," said Jansen. "I was winning all season so easily. . . by three or four tenths of a second. . . which in speed skating is a very large margin. I don't think I lost more than one race during the entire season leading to the Lillehammer Olympics."

Jansen started off quickly in the 500 meters. "The first turn was very good for me," Jansen remembered. "As far as I was concerned after that the race was mine because I always pull away from everybody in the last half of the race."

In the stands Robin, his wife of three years, was cheering him on. Robin's mother alongside was holding their nine-month-old daughter, Jane, named after Jansen's sister, who ironically died six years ago this day.

"I thought he looked great," remembered Robin. "Then on the last turn I saw the ice fly and I knew he slipped. I turned to my mother and screamed, 'I can't believe this is happening again!'"

The slip was costly. When the final skaters had finished, Jansen was in eighth place.

Four days later, the 1,000 meters was scheduled, the last race of his Olympic career.

"I was not confident. I didn't feel good. My skates weren't gripping the ice properly," said Jansen. "All I could think of was 'this will be over soon. In a minute and a half it will be done.'"

The rest was Olympic history. Dan Jansen skated the greatest race of his career even though he had a slight slip on the next to last turn. When he crossed the finish line he had broken the previous world record by eleven-hundredths of a second.

On the victory platform Jansen had remembrances of the past.

"I was hoping the national anthem would never end. My whole life passed by me. . . my family, Robin. . . my daughter Jane. . . and of course my sister Jane. . . And as the anthem was nearing its end, I was trying to think of saying something to Jane. So I looked up and gave a little salute. . . for the whole Dan Jansen story began with her death and now it could finally end."

Afterward Jansen took a victory lap. Moving around the track he glided toward the stands. His daughter Jane was handed to him, and now smiling, the two moved around the track to the thunderous cheers of the thousands who remained to say their final farewell to this courageous athlete.

Dan Jansen had fulfilled what he always intended to do. The words: "I do not try to be better than anybody else. I only try to be better than myself."

Jeff Farrell Rome, 1960

In the spring of 1960, Jeff Farrell of the United States looked forward to the Olympic trials in swimming, since it was expected that he would be the favorite to win three gold medals — in the 100 meter freestyle and as the anchor man of the 4 x 100 medley relay and 4 x 200 freestyle relay.

The predictions of a successful Olympics for Farrell were based on the fact that he held the best time in the world in the 100 meter freestyle and was equally superb in the 200 meter freestyle. Though the 200 meter freestyle was not on the Olympic program, it was a scheduled event in the United States trials in order to select the 4 x 200 Olympic relay team.

Six days before the Olympic trials were scheduled, Farrell awoke in the middle of the night with intense stomach pains. He writhed around for hours rather than bother his room-mate. Finally the pain was too much. Farrell was rushed to the hospital, where an immediate examination revealed that his appendix had burst. An emergency operation saved his life.

The United States Olympic Committee was in a dilemma. America's finest swimmer was severely handicapped. In an unprecedented decision they decided that they would waive his appearance at the trials and permit him to qualify two weeks later. Farrell declined this special consideration.

Six days after his operation Jeff Farrell appeared at the trials for the final of the 100 meter freestyle final. The stitches from his appendectomy had not been removed. Incredibly, Farrell won a berth in the final after swimming in qualifying and semi-final heats.

Though the final was close, Farrell finished third behind Lance Larson and Bruce Hunter. In 1960 only the first two

finishers qualified for the 100 meter Olympic freestyle.

"I was quite depressed afterward," recalled Farrell. "I lost out by a tenth of a second. A few meters from the finish I got tangled up in one of the lane ropes and it probably cost me half a second."

A few days later the 200 meter freestyle was scheduled to select the relay team. Again, Farrell made it to the final.

The crowd roared as the swimmers reacted to the starter's gun.

"I missed the 100 meter freestyle team by inches," recalled Farrell. "In the 200 meters I thought I had a chance to win."

All eyes were on Farrell as the swimmers thrashed through the water. One newspaper columnist wrote afterward, "Never had so many spectators been cheering for a man to finish sixth."

Farrell did better than that. He finished fourth in the 200 meters and now was in a good position to be selected for both relay teams.

As the Rome Olympics approached, Farrell returned to his pre-operation form, so much so that his teammate, Bruce Hunter, offered him his spot on the 100 meter freestyle team.

"It was a magnificent gesture," recalled Farrell. "But Bruce won his spot fair and square. I was not going to take it away from him."

The amazing saga of Jeff Farrell reached its climax at the Rome Olympics. There Farrell anchored both United States relay teams to two Olympic gold medals and two world records.

Jeff Farrell — who had to qualify at the Olympic trials six days after an emergency appendectomy — competing in the 1960 Games in Rome (below), and as member of the gold medal winning 4 x 100 meter medley relay team (far right).

Yasuhiro Yamashita
Los Angeles, 1984

Japan

At 5:00 p.m., August 11, 1984, more than 4,000 spectators filled the arena at the Los Angeles Olympics to witness the open division judo championship that would feature one of the greatest athletes in modern sport — Yasuhiro Yamashita of Japan.

Yamashita is a national hero in Japan, where the sport began over a century ago. Translated, judo means "the gentle way." Pupils are taught to emphasize strength, technique and concentration as opposed to violence. Judo players are told that "yielding is strength. Gentle turns away sturdy. Bend like a bamboo, then strike back."

Leading to Los Angeles, Yamashita had a string of 194 straight victories over a seven year period. During this period he won the All Japan Judo Championship eight times and the world championships four successive times. His opponents consider him unbeatable. Judo experts consider him invincible. Standing five feet eleven inches, he had one more goal.

"I have wanted to win an Olympic gold medal since I was a child. I missed an opportunity in 1980 when the boycott prevented me from competing in the Moscow Olympics," recalled Yamashita.

Most of Yamashita's victories during his streak have been won by "ippons," the equivalent in judo to a knockout in boxing. His bouts usually last less than a minute.

He won his first bout in less than 30 seconds, but one hour later, in defeating Arthur Schnabel of West Germany, Yamashita severely injured a muscle in his right leg. He left the mat limping and in great pain.

Less than an hour later he faced Laurent del Colombo of France. The rules of judo are strange to the uninitiated. It is not considered improper for an opponent to attack an injury. Yamashita knows this, repeatedly warding off his opponent's attack to his injury.

In the early part of the bout del Colombo almost scored an ippon, but Yamashita escapes. Less than a minute later Yamashita scored his own ippon and now had moved into the final.

His opponent was Mohamed Rashwan of Egypt, who had won all three of his previous bouts easily. All three wins have been by ippons.

"In my semi-final, it was the first time I ever thought I might lose," said Yamashita later. "My injury was very painful and prevented my normal movement. But I must forget the pain for my last fight."

Yamashita was spectacular, confidently deflecting the

powerful blows to his injured leg. After but a few seconds, he threw Rashwan to the mat, then slowly lowered his body atop the Egyptian. Rashwan was helpless. The referee raised his hand in signal of victory. Yasuhiro had won the gold medal. He had fulfilled the philosophy of judo: "Yielding is strength. Gentle turns away sturdy."

190

Joan Benoit Los Angeles, 1984

What a difference 56 years makes. At the 1928 Amsterdam Olympics, several women collapsed at the finish of the 800 meter run and had to be treated for exhaustion.

The photographs of the event showed a few women gasping for breath, which brought forth drastic action by the International Amateur Athletic Federation. It was decided that, for their own safety, women could not compete in distances longer than 200 meters at the Olympics.

On the morning of August 5, 1984, more than a half century later, 80,000 spectators in the Los Angeles Coliseum were wildly cheering the gray-uniformed runner wearing a white cap as she emerged from the archway on to the track. In advance the loudspeaker had informed the spectators that the runner was Joan Benoit of the United States. This was the climax to the 26 mile, 385 yard run — the first women's Olympic marathon ever, the longest event on the track and field program.

As she crossed the finish line and waved to the cheering throng, only a few knew that Joan Benoit would become part of not only Olympic history, but also medical history. For her story would not be believed if presented as a piece of fiction.

The United States Olympic women's marathon trials were contested on May 12, 1984, just eleven weeks before the Olympic competition. The first three women finishers in this harshest of track and field events would represent the United States.

One year before the trials, Benoit had come back from double Achilles surgery to become one of the favorites to represent the United States.

However, less than two months before the Olympic trials, Benoit began to have pains in her right knee so severe that her normal running motion was impaired. Soon the knee completely locked and her doctor administered cortisone injections.

The treatment worked for a time, but the pain recurred. Benoit not only could not run — she could barely walk.

On April 25, just seventeen days before the Olympic trials, the decision was made. Normal surgery would not have allowed her to recover in time for the trials. She decided to undergo arthroscopic surgery.

Five days later she tested the leg. There was no pain. However, she was overcompensating. The result was a painful hamstring injury to her left leg. On May 5, one week before the trials, Benoit was prepared to give up. Nevertheless, she continued to have her legs treated, and on the morning of May 12 she decided to give it a try. She would start the race and run as far as she could. Joan Benoit won the trials seventeen days after her operation.

The climax to the story came on August 5, when Joan took a victory lap around the Los Angeles Coliseum, waving an American flag to an adoring crowd, the winner of the first women's Olympic marathon gold medal.

Murray Rose & Tsuyoshi Yamanaka

Melbourne, 1956   Australia/Japan

No one could predict that the 1956 Melbourne Olympic 1,500 meter freestyle swimming final would be the most dramatic event of the Games. It would be another confrontation between two great young swimmers — seventeen-

MURRAY ROSE

year-old Murray Rose of Australia and seventeen-year-old Tsuyoshi Yamanaka of Japan, who ironically were born twelve days apart.

Though they were good friends because of the many times they met each other at the pool, and would later become closer as teammates at USC, Rose and Yamanaka never gave any evidence of their friendship in public.

World War II had been over only eleven years and there were still remembrances in Australia of the war years when their country was in danger of being invaded by Japan.

Both Rose and Yamanaka were national heroes in their own countries. They would meet twice in Melbourne in the 400 and 1,500 meter freestyle events.

A few days before the 1,500 meters, Rose defeated Yamanaka in the 400 meter freestyle. But the 1,500 meters has always been considered the classic swimming event — the longest race on the program and a test of strength, speed and endurance.

At the start, neither would look at the other. When the gun sent them off, the thousands in the stands knew that it would be a two-man race, even though George Breen of the United States had created a world record in his qualifying heat.

The race was a close one but with each lap Rose moved farther and farther ahead. With 100 meters left in the race, Rose was in front by six meters. It was then that Yamanaka started a furious finishing kick.

Yamanaka kept cutting down the distance but it was not enough. Rose won by two meters and the Australian crowd went wild with joy.

"We looked at each other for a few seconds," remembered Rose. "For years there was still some resentment in Australia towards the Japanese. I knew the crowd was watching us closely. Then, simultaneously we both smiled, fell over the lane lines and warmly embraced. Behind us we heard the crowd cheering. But the true significance of our race and what happened afterward was on the front page of every newspaper the next day. One of the captions read, 'The war is finally over.'"

But, even more dramatic was the incredible fact that the 1,500 meter race took place on December 7, 1956 — exactly fifteen years to the day of the Japanese attack on Pearl Harbor and the subsequent declaration of war against the United States, Australia and its allies.

There was one additional honor for Murray Rose. As a member of the 4 x 200 meter relay team which won the gold, his three victories made him the youngest male triple gold medal winner in Olympic swimming history.

USA-USSR Basketball Munich, 1972

The greatest basketball controversy in the history of the Olympics took place at the 1972 Munich Games — the final between the United States and the Soviet Union.

Leading to this final, the United States had won every gold medal since basketball was added to the Olympic program in 1936 at the Berlin Games. U.S. teams were undefeated in 62 straight games over eight Olympic competitions.

On the evening of September 9, 11:45 p.m. Munich time, the final took place. It was postponed one day due to a moratorium of Olympic competition in memory of the murder of eleven Israeli athletes a few days earlier.

In Munich both the United States and the Soviet Union had unblemished records — each winning eight straight games. Nevertheless, every expert predicted that the outcome of the final was not in doubt. The only question was how big a margin the United States' victory would be.

The game did not go as the Americans expected. With ten minutes to play, the Soviet Union led 38 to 28. The United States kept chipping away and trailed 49 to 48 when, with six seconds left in the game, Doug Collins of the U.S. picked up a loose ball at mid-court and drove for the basket. He missed the layup but was fouled and awarded two shots. The official clock showed three seconds left in the game.

Collins sunk both shots and the United States led 50 to 49. The Soviets put the ball in play. The ball got to mid-court when the referee's whistle blew with one second left.

A conference was held at the scorer's table and it was decided that even though the Soviets had called an illegal time out, they would be given a second opportunity to throw the ball in. The timekeeper was ordered to reset the clock to show three seconds left.

The Soviets threw the ball in and took a long, desperate shot from mid-court. It missed. The buzzer sounded and the United States apparently won 50 to 49.

The Soviets again converged on the scorer's table and

Strong emotions are displayed on the court (above) after a series of incredible officials' decisions at the end of the United States versus the Soviet Union basketball final allowed a 51-50 Soviet victory to be upheld.

protested that the clock was not set back to the original three seconds. A high technical basketball official in no way connected with the actual game agreed. He ordered the referee and timekeeper to reset the clock to the original three seconds.

The Americans protested to no avail. For the third time the Soviets were able to put the ball in play. A long full court toss was thrown to 6 foot 8 inch Soviet forward Alexander Belov underneath the basket. Belov caught the ball between the desperate attempts of two American defenders to block it. Belov easily laid the ball up. The buzzer sounded with the Soviets in front 51 to 50.

The United States protested and petitioned the International Olympic Committee with sworn statements by the referee and timekeeper that the Soviet victory was illegal.

More than four months after the controversy the IOC handed down its final decision. The United States protest was denied and the Soviet Union was the winner of the gold medal.

Perhaps the most dramatic remembrance of the great controversy remains with the photograph of the medal awards ceremony. Standing on the top step of the victory podium is the Soviet team and to their left is the team from Cuba, the bronze medal winner. The silver medal level is empty. The United States team refused to appear and to this day none of the players on the team have accepted their second place medals.

Mark Spitz

United States

Mark Spitz created Olympic history at the 1972 Munich Games by winning seven gold medals in swimming, all world records — four individual events and three relays. Years later I learned that Spitz almost lost his chance at Olympic immortality.

Four years earlier in Mexico City at the 1968 Games, the eighteen-year-old Spitz predicted he would win five gold medals. By his standards he failed miserably. He didn't win any of his individual events, but garnered two gold medals in the relays.

Before the 1972 Munich Games, many predicted that the 22-year-old Spitz would make up for his previous Olympic failure by winning all seven events he entered.

Spitz made the experts look good immediately in his first event in Munich by easily winning the 200 meter butterfly. A few hours later Spitz swam the anchor leg in the 4 x 100 meter freestyle relay for his second gold medal. But when the individual 100 meter times for each of the Americans were released, Spitz teammate and chief rival in the 100 meters, Jerry Heidenreich, swam his third leg twelve hundredths of a second faster than Spitz's leg. Some experts predicted that Heidenreich would beat Spitz in the 100 meter freestyle later in the week.

In the next three days Spitz easily won the 200 meter freestyle and the 100 meter butterfly. In four races Spitz had won four gold medals and four world records had been created.

One hour later the streak continued. Spitz swam the anchor leg for the American 4 x 200 relay team for his fifth gold medal and fifth world record.

It was then that Spitz had a conversation with his coach, Sherm Chavoor. "I told the coach that I had won five races and was very tired," Spitz recalled. "So I said, 'Coach, I think it would be better if I scratched from the 100 meter freestyle and saved myself for the 4 x 100 medley relay. Six gold medals isn't so bad.'"

"You mean five gold medals," said Chavoor with sarcasm.

"What do you mean?" said Spitz.

"Listen, Mark, if you don't swim the 100 meters, you're out of the relay. You might as well go home now," Chavoor said. "They'll say you're 'chicken' — that you're afraid to face Jerry Heidenreich."

Spitz knew that Coach Chavoor was in earnest. He entered the 100 meters and beat Heidenreich by a few feet and then climaxed a brilliant seven gold medal, seven world record performance as part of the victorious 4 x 100 medley relay team in the final event of the swimming program.

Before the podium ceremony his three teammates lifted Spitz to their shoulders and took a victory lap around the pool. Spitz had this photograph framed.

"That picture with my teammates holding me high above them I enjoy more than the one that was taken with the seven gold medals around my neck," smiled Spitz. "Having a tribute from your teammates is a feeling that can never be duplicated."

Betty Cuthbert

Melbourne, 1956; Tokyo, 1964   Australia

Arguably the most obscure "immortal" in the history of women's track and field is Betty Cuthbert of Australia.

At the 1956 Melbourne Olympics, the beautiful, blond eighteen-year-old Cuthbert became the female star of the Games. But with no worldwide television to inform the world of her greatness, her exploits were confined to limited newspaper reportage.

Cuthbert was entered in three events — the 100 meters, 200 meters and 4 x 100 relay.

In the final of the 100 meters, Cuthbert was not the favorite. This role was assigned to her teammate, Marlene Mathews.

"Marlene constantly beat me in the 100 and 200 meters," remembered Cuthbert. "Then, about six months before the Olympics, I began to beat her a few times. But the day of the Olympic final she was the favorite."

Cuthbert won the 100 meters easily, followed by Christa Stubnick of Germany, with Marlene Mathews of Australia third.

"It was very exciting because the 100 meters was not my favorite event," Cuthbert recalled. "I love the 200 and thought I had a good chance in that one."

Betty was correct. She came down the stretch to win by a few feet in a finish that was a carbon copy of the 100 meters. Stubnick of Germany was second and Marlene Mathews, Australia, third. Cuthbert had now endeared herself to all of Australia, for four years earlier in Helsinki, Marjorie Jackson of Australia won those two same events.

A few days later Betty anchored the Australian 4 x 100 relay team to victory to win her third gold. There were already predictions that she would duplicate this feat four years later at the 1960 Rome Olympics.

But for Betty Cuthbert, Rome was a nightmare. A few months before the Games got underway Betty pulled a hamstring in her leg. She thought it had healed, but it acted up in the second round of the 100 meters and she was eliminated. The injury caused her to withdraw from the 200 meters and 4 x 100 relay. America's Wilma Rudolph, with three gold medals, had supplanted Australia's Golden Girl as the world's fastest woman. For all practical purposes Betty Cuthbert's Olympic career was over.

"I retired in 1960 for the simple reason I thought I had done enough," Cuthbert recalled. "But then this little voice in my head kept waking me up every night and telling me I should run again. People thought I was crazy when I told them about the 'little voice.' But I kept hearing it. So then I made the decision to try again at the 1964 Tokyo Games and immediately I was able to sleep. The voice stopped talking to me."

The event she chose was the 400 meters. Betty was not the favorite. She had finished third in her qualifying heat and second in the semi-final. The gold medal was expected to be a duel between Ann Packer of Great Britain and Betty's teammate, Judith Amoore. For Cuthbert, who is a sprinter, this was a new event. She had the speed to win, but was uncertain about her ability to last the distance.

Cuthbert got off quickly into the lead and after the first 200 meters was in front by three meters. She maintained her lead into the final stretch, but then Ann Packer of Great Britain, the winner of the 800 meter gold medal, started her drive. Packer slowly cut down the distance. But it was not enough. Cuthbert crossed the finish line two feet in front.

Betty Cuthbert had done what many thought impossible. Eight years after winning three gold medals, she had won a fourth.

Greg Barton Seoul, 1988   United States

At 9:00 a.m., Saturday, October 1, 1988, thousands of spectators gathered at the Han River Regatta course to witness the 1,000 meter singles kayak final at the Seoul Olympic Games. After a series of qualifying and semi-final heats, nine men had made it to the final.

One of the favorites in the race was 28-year-old Greg Barton of the United States. It was predicted that his main opposition would come from Grant Davies of Australia and defending Olympic champion Alan Thompson of New Zealand.

Barton's task was a formidable one. Kayaking had been put on the Olympic program in the 1936 Berlin Games but since then, in the more than a half century of competition, no American had ever won a gold medal.

Greg Barton is a unique Olympian. He is a mechanical engineer, a summa cum laude graduate from the University of Michigan. As a child he had daily chores on his parents' farm in Homer, Michigan, a town with a population of 2,000. It was there he gained the strength to compete in athletics, for Greg Barton had a physical handicap. He was born with a club foot.

"With all the surgery and physical problems I went through," said Barton, "I think it made me tougher mentally. When the training was getting tough, I would say to myself, 'This is not as tough as what I had to endure to get here.'"

The 1,000 meter race was a close one throughout. Barton stayed near the leaders, then with 200 meters left, he took the lead. As he approached the finish line, Grant Davies of Australia made his move and both crossed the finish line as one. Neither knew who was the winner.

Barton paddled to meet his teammate, Norm Bellingham, whom he would join in the doubles final scheduled a little more than an hour later.

"The scoreboard flashed that Davies had beaten me by thirty-seven-hundredths of a second," said Barton, "and I was resigned that I had won the silver medal."

But the officials had made a mistake. After a long delay and with meticulous viewing of the electronic finish photograph, the scoreboard flashed the news. Barton has won by one hundredth of a second.

Barton did not have time to celebrate, since he and Bellingham had to get ready for the 1,000 meter doubles. The Americans were not expected to win. Their main rival was the legendary New Zealand pair of Paul MacDonald and Ian Ferguson, who four years earlier in Los Angeles were multiple gold medal winners. Ironically, Bellingham trained under the supervision of the Kiwis for three years.

With 200 meters left in the race, New Zealand led, followed by Australia. Barton and Bellingham were in third place. But now the Americans started to sprint, and they closed the distance from the leaders. The finish was almost as close at Barton's victory in the singles. The Americans defeated New Zealand by twenty-nine-hundredths of a second.

By a combined total margin of thirty-hundredths of a second, Greg Barton had made Olympic history — the first American to win a kayak Olympic gold medal and the first kayaker in history to win two gold medals in 90 minutes.

Eleanor Holm

Los Angeles, 1932; Berlin, 1936

United States

America's Eleanor Holm has a unique Olympic association. She is perhaps the only Olympian who became an international celebrity by not competing — more so than when she won an Olympic gold medal.

As "the baby" of the 1928 Olympic team in Amsterdam, fourteen-year-old Eleanor Holm finished fifth in the 100 meter backstroke.

Four years later at the 1932 Los Angeles Games, Eleanor was the finest backstroker in the world. In an informal poll she was also voted the most beautiful and graceful athlete of the Games — constantly being sought out by the press and motion picture scouts.

When she won the 100 meter backstroke at the Los Angeles Games, she was besieged with motion picture offers. Instead, she married the popular band leader Art Jarrett and became a singer with his band. Between the 1932 Games and the upcoming 1936 Berlin Olympics she was a social butterfly with a contrasting lifestyle. In the evenings she would accompany her husband on their nightclub dates and by day she would stay in shape at gymnasiums and pools in whatever city she was in.

Though Eleanor was not the "typical" amateur of the 1930s, she was still America's greatest female backstroker and an early favorite to repeat her gold medal victory at the 1936 Berlin Games.

Even though she was the glamour girl of the team, she was loved by her fellow athletes — mostly for her earthiness and independence.

Aboard the SS *Manhattan* that was taking the 1936 United States team to Berlin, Eleanor was not used to the confinement of the athletes' quarters.

Certain of her status, she roamed the upper decks where the officials were quartered and was constantly seen partaking in public displays of drinking — both wine and champagne. Eleanor paid no heed to the reprimands.

While still at sea, the United States Olympic Committee issued a bulletin that Eleanor had been removed from the team. Eleanor tried to convince USOC President Avery Brundage that she was just adhering to the rules and regulations that was the "bible" to team members.

"The regulations stated," said Eleanor, "that all team members should continue the same training preparations that we were accustomed to having in the States. That's all I was doing. At home it was my custom to have a glass of wine or champagne every day after a workout."

What was logical to Eleanor made no impression on the USOC. Despite petitions from many of her fellow athletes for her reinstatement, she was barred from the competition.

"I'm still very bitter about what Avery Brundage did," said Eleanor sadly. "He not only lost a certain gold medal for me, but a gold medal for the United States. But I got even with him. The Germans couldn't understand how they would do such a thing, so I was invited to all the Embassy parties as their guest. And whenever Mr. Brundage showed up he would stay a few minutes, then leave with the maddest look on his face. He didn't like the fact that all the photographers were taking pictures of me and not him."

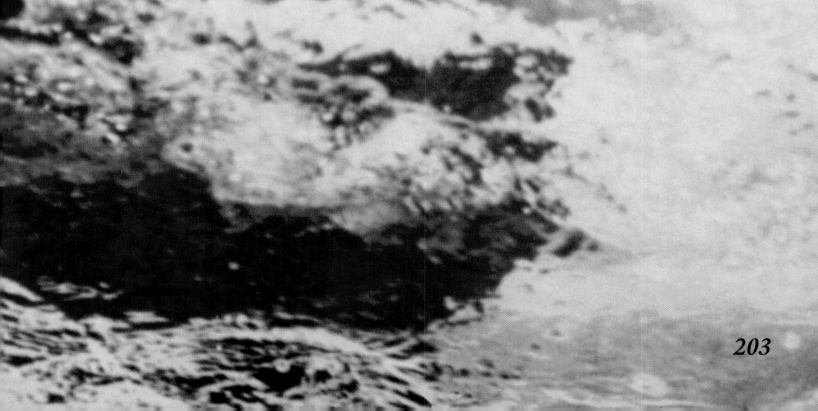

Lawrence Lemieux Seoul, 1988

On September 24, 1988, the sailing competition was underway at Pusan, 32 kilometers from South Korea's capital of Seoul, the main Olympic site. The conditions for sailing had unexpectedly become dangerous. Acceptable winds of fifteen knots per hour had escalated at times to 35 knots. The waters were playing havoc with boats and crews. In the 470 class, two sailors on the Singapore team, Joseph Chan and Shaw Her Siew, were thrown into the water, suffering injuries and unable to right their boat. The situation was a dangerous one.

Sailing alone near the half point in his race on the nearby Finn class race course was Lawrence Lemieux of Edmonton, Canada. Lemieux was then in second place in this, the fifth race of a seven race event and was given a good chance to win one of the medals.

Lemieux immediately took action, forgetting his own race and sailing toward Joseph Chan in the 470 class. As the Canadian was dragging Chan aboard, his own boat began filling with water. Successfully rescuing Chan, Lemieux immediately headed toward Shaw Her Siew, who was clinging tenaciously to his overturned boat. Lemieux performed the same rescue operation and now both Singapore sailors were in his boat. But for Lemieux victory was impossible. He waited for an official patrol boat to reach him, then transferred the two men.

Then Lemieux continued in his race, but the loss of time during the rescue operation put him out of contention. He finished 22nd in a race that started with 32 boats.

Soon after the race, the story of the rescue reached the jury of the International Yacht Racing Union. They unanimously decided that Lemieux should be awarded second place for this, the fifth race — the position he was in when he went to the aid of the Singapore crew. None of the other contestants questioned the decision.

Though Lemieux did not win a medal in the overall seven race competition, at the medal awards ceremony Juan Antonio Samaranch, President of the International Olympic Committee, paid honor to Lemieux for his act.

"By your sportsmanship, self-sacrifice and courage," said Samaranch, "you embody all that is right with the Olympic ideal."

205

John Ian Wing

Melbourne, 1956

Australia

Seventeen-year-old John Ian Wing, an Australian of Chinese parentage, was an Olympic champion at the 1956 Melbourne Olympic Games. He didn't win a gold medal and he didn't compete in any of the athletic competitions. All John Ian Wing did was to write a simple, poignant letter to the Melbourne Olympic Organizing Committee and because of it changed the look of the Games forever.

Leading to the 1956 Melbourne Games there was much strife in the world The Hungarian revolt became bloody when the Soviet Union sent troops and tanks into Budapest, even as its Olympic team was making its way to Melbourne.

Nevertheless, the Games were a smashing success.

A few days after the opening ceremonies, Sir Wilfred Kent Hughes, the head of the Melbourne Olympic Organizing Committee, received a handwritten letter. The fact that he had time to read it was as improbable as to what happened as a result of it.

"Dear Friends," the letter began.

"I am a Chinese boy and have just turned 17 years of age. Before the Games I thought everything would be in a muddle. However, I am quite wrong. It is the most successful Games ever staged. . . Mr. Hughes, I believe it has been suggested a march be put on during the closing ceremonies and you said it couldn't be done. I think it can be done. . . the march I have in mind is different than the one during the Opening Ceremony. . . During the march there will be only one nation. . . what more could anybody want if the whole world could be made as one nation. . . "

It was signed, "John Ian Wing."

So it was done. And thus began a tradition at the Melbourne Cricket Ground that would remain for all the Olympic Games that were to come. . . men and women athletes from many nations saying a final farewell as one nation, as opposed to marching under their own national flag.

And for Australia, it was right and proper that such a tradi-tion should start in Melbourne. For this beautiful land that lies between the Southern Cross did honor to these Games that the ancient Greeks called the Truce of Gods. For those who were there would witness a mixture of love and warmth that had not been seen before, nor had been felt since.

The Melbourne Olympic Committee had paid notice to the simple letter of John Ian Wing, but unfortunately he was not among the many thousands who were there to witness it.

As the athletes marched into the stadium the massed bands struck up the beloved "Waltzing Matilda." The crowd roared its acclaim. The athletes waved to the cheering throng as a chorus of hundreds sang words that were specially written for the final march. Feelings that were expressed in the Aboriginal words of good-bye to a loved one, "Momok Wonargo Ora Go–Yai. . . Farewell, Brother, by and by come back."

As the athletes made their way around the stadium, the voices resounded through the stadium.

"Homeward, homeward, soon you will be
   going now.
MOMOK WONARGO ORA GO-YAI
Joy of our meeting, Pain of our parting
Shine in our eyes as we bid you goodbye
Goodbye Olympians, goodbye Olympians,
On comes the Evening, West goes the Day
Roll up your swags and pack them full
   of memories
Fair be the wind as you speed on your way."

Then, as one final, emotional tribute, the chorus sang the magnificent Scottish song of farewell:

"Will ye no' come back again?
Will ye no' come back again?
Will ye no' come back again?
Better lov'd ye Canna be. . .
Will ye no' come back again. . . "

With every ending there is a new beginning. John Ian Wing's letter had changed the closing ceremonies forever.

Mike Boit
Montreal, 1976

 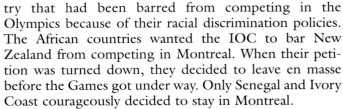

On the morning of the opening day ceremonies of the 1976 Montreal Olympic Games, Mike Boit, Kenya's great middle distance runner and one of the favorites to win the 800 meters scheduled for a few days later, came into my hotel room and stood silently in front of me.

"Hi, Mike," I said with a smile. Boit stared at me sadly, then looked down. I knew he had been crying.

"I came to say goodbye," Mike said, unable to look at me.

The day before Mike heard the news. Kenya had joined the African boycott of the Montreal Games in protest to the New Zealand rugby team months earlier accepting an invitation to play in South Africa — a country that had been barred from competing in the Olympics because of their racial discrimination policies. The African countries wanted the IOC to bar New Zealand from competing in Montreal. When their petition was turned down, they decided to leave en masse before the Games got under way. Only Senegal and Ivory Coast courageously decided to stay in Montreal.

Boit was looking forward to what was being predicted as one of the great 800 meter finals in Olympic history, when he would face Alberto Juantorena of Cuba and Rick Wohlhuter of the United States.

Mike and I talked about how unfair it was to the African athletes that their officials had made such a catastrophic decision. Still looking down, Mike sadly nodded.

"Mike," I said, "we have an extra hotel room that's not being used. You don't have to go home with the team. I want you to be our guest during the Games."

Mike looked up and for the first time he smiled.

"You won't get in any trouble if you stay?" I asked.

"I don't care," said Mike, and he threw his arms around me in a warm embrace.

A few days later Mike sat next to me as the finalists for the 800 meters stepped onto the track. Four years earlier in Munich he won the bronze medal in this event, one tenth of a second behind the winner, Dave Wottle of the United States and Yevgeni Arzhanov of the Soviet Union in a photo finish.

Mike stared intently as the runners went off in the 800 meter final. Every few seconds I would turn to Mike, but he was expressionless. I knew he was going through the race as if he was in it.

As Juantorena finally took over the lead with incredible ease, Mike's head moved forward as if he was moving with the great Cuban champion.

When Juantorena crossed the finish line an easy winner, Mike's eyes followed him as the Cuban waved to a cheering crowd. History had been made. Juantorena had set a world record and in doing so became the first gold medalist from a non–English speaking country in the 800 meters.

Mike was silent as Juantorena continued around the track in a victory lap.

"Do you think you could have won?" I asked. There was a pause and tears started down his face as he nodded. "We'll never know, will we?" he said. "We'll never know."

Eamonn Coghlan

If an athlete were ever to be considered the perfect symbol of the Olympic philosophy "to enter the arena. . . make the attempt and pursue excellence," then Eamonn Coghlan of Ireland would be the unanimous choice.

At the 1976 Games in Montreal, with one lap to go, 23-year-old Eamonn Coghlan was in the lead in the 1,500 meters. It appeared he would win one of the medals, but with 250 meters left in the race, Coghlan was passed by three runners and finished fourth.

Immediately after the event, Coghlan looked forward to the 1980 Moscow Games, where he would try a new event — the 5,000 meters. A few weeks before the Moscow Games, Coghlan, again a favorite to win a medal, was hit by the stomach flu. His training was intermittent, yet he qualified for the 5,000 meter final.

Again Coghlan was in contention, but in the final lap three runners passed him and again he had to settle for fourth place.

In the following years, emotional and physical misfortune followed him. He lost a year of training and competition due to a stress fracture of his leg, and within a short space of time the three most influential men in his life died — his father, his high school coach Gerry Farnan and Jumbo Elliott, his legendary coach at Villanova.

Early in 1983 he set the world indoor mile record (which still stands today), but his major sights were focused on winning a world championship. He entered the 5,000 meter race to be held at the 1983 world championships in Helsinki.

Before leaving for Helsinki, Coghlan visited the grave of Gerry Farnan, his beloved high school coach.

"I went over to Gerry's grave to say a few prayers, and I saw the epitaph on his stone," recalled Coghlan. "I had never read it before, even though I visited the grave site many times. It read, 'Don't quit when you're beaten. Fight back to an even more glorious victory. Not only in competition, but in life.' I plucked some grass from in front of the grave and stuck it in my wallet. I took it with me and said to myself, 'Gerry, on the day of the final, you're going to be with me.'"

Coghlan fulfilled his dream. He won the 5,000 meter world championship and became one of the favorites to win a medal at the 1984 Los Angeles Olympics. But again tragedy struck. The stress fracture in his shin bone returned and he could not compete at the 1984 Olympics.

In 1988 the Irish Olympic Committee did not consider Coghlan's performances worthy of making the Olympic team for the Seoul Games. Coghlan persisted in his training, overcame the politics within the Irish Olympic Committee and was finally named to the team.

At age 35, in the summer of 1988, Coghlan faced the starter's pistol for the 5,000 meters semi-final race. Coghlan was among the leaders during the early part of the race, but soon he began to fall back and it was apparent that his chances were over. With each lap he fell farther and farther behind, but he would not quit. He finished 28th out of 30 starters and did not qualify for the final. After the race, Coghlan, in the tradition of the great Irish poets, said:

"I said to myself, I'm not going to quit. . . I'm not going to quit here in the Olympic Games. I'm going to see it through to the end. . . You go to the Olympic Games to compete, you don't go to the Olympic Games to quit.

"I can hold my head up high, I think, for the rest of my life and say, I really tried. I tried honestly. I tried fairly. I had a tremendous life out of my sport, but it wasn't to be. I went to the Olympic Games because that's what it's all about. Making the effort. . . being a sportsman. . . being a true sportsman."

Bonnie Blair

Calgary, 1988; Albertville, 1992; Lillehammer, 1992

United States

On March 18, 1964, Charlie Blair was watching five of his children compete in a speed skating contest at a local arena in their hometown of Champaign, Illinois. Charlie was nervous. His wife, Eleanor, was expecting their sixth child.

"In those days husbands really weren't allowed in the delivery room," laughed Bonnie Blair. "So Dad figured that instead of waiting for me to be born, since Mom had been through this five times before, that he'd take the rest of the kids to a skating meet. . . And then it was announced that another 'Blair girl' had been added to the speed skating world. So I was just a few hours old when I got my first loudspeaker announcement."

Bonnie Blair was nineteen when she competed in the Olympics for the first time at the 1984 Sarajevo Games. She finished eighth in the 500 meters. Her appearance there was witnessed by her mother and two sisters — the beginning of a saga that the speed skating world would know as "the Blair Bunch," the network of family and friends that would follow Bonnie through innumerable Olympic, world and national championships.

At the Calgary 1988 Games about thirty of the Blair Bunch showed up to watch Bonnie test her skills against the then incomparable East Germans.

In the second pairing of the 500 meters, Christa Rothenburger of East Germany broke her own world record and appeared certain that she would successfully defend the title she won four years earlier in Sarajevo.

But two pairs later Bonnie Blair broke Rothenburger's record by two hundredths of a second and the mystique of the East Germans had been shattered.

"It was so thrilling," recalled Eleanor Blair, the matriarch of the Blair Bunch. "My husband, Charlie, was there to witness it. He was suffering from cancer and died soon after.

But he was there to see Bonnie's first gold medal. It was very, very special."

Four years later in Albertville, about 45 of the Blair Bunch came to watch Bonnie win her second and third gold medals in the 500 and 1,000 meters.

"You know, a lot of people think that I'm under a lot of pressure with my family and friends spending all that money to follow me around," said Bonnie. "But, you know, they don't care whether I win or lose. They'd come anyway 'cause we're one big family that's having lots of fun. . . "

More than 60 of the Blair Bunch came to Lillehammer in 1994 to perhaps witness history. If Bonnie won the 500 meters, she'd become the first speed skater, male or female, to win three successive gold medals in the same event.

Bonnie skated in the third pair and was spectacular. She easily went into first place. Bonnie was still in the lead when there was an intermission in order for the ice to be resurfaced. There were eleven heats still to be contested. Bonnie then broke precedent. With the event still on, she decided to celebrate.

"I wanted to hug my mom and the rest of my family and friends," she laughed. "It didn't matter that the competition wasn't over. I just wanted to be with them."

Bonnie Blair had no fears. When the competition resumed, no one could come near her time. She had made Olympic history with her third successive 500 meter gold medal.

A few days later she won the 1,000 meters for the second time. . . the last race of her Olympic career.

After the victory platform ceremony Bonnie took a victory lap for the final time at the Olympic Games. As she circled the track, one columnist was writing the lead to his story: "Throughout history many Olympic heroes have been created. Bonnie Blair invented herself."

Emil Zátopek
London, 1948; Helsinki, 1952;   Czechoslovakia

Emil Zátopek of Czechoslovakia will never forget July 24, 1952, at the Helsinki Olympic Stadium. The great Czech distance runner had just won the 5,000 meters, his third Olympic gold medal. A few days earlier, he won the 10,000 meters to go along with the gold and silver he won in the 10,000 meters and 5,000 meters four years earlier in London.

Now here in Helsinki as he left the 5,000 meter platform ceremony in which the Czech national anthem was played in his honor, Zátopek noticed that the women entrants for the javelin were entering the field.

He rushed over to his wife, Dana, one of the contestants. Proudly he showed her his latest gold medal.

"Emil, let me have it, I will hold it for good luck," she said. Emil handed it to her.

On her first throw, Dana broke the Olympic record and her effort held up throughout the rest of the competition. The Zátopeks became the first and only married couple ever to win Olympic gold medals on the same day in separate events.

The Zátopeks celebrated their double victory that night. Dana was exuberant and content to savor the victory during the remaining days in Helsinki. But Emil was bored. Though he was already the hero of the Games with his great victories in the 10,000 and 5,000 meters, he was tired of the meetings with the press.

At one interview he told a surprised reporter, "I think I'll try the marathon."

So on the final day of the track and field competition he lined up for the 26 mile 385 yard classic event, a race he had never run before.

"I was told that Jim Peters of Great Britain was the heavy favorite to win the marathon," said Zátopek, "So before the race, I introduced myself to him and asked if he would mind if I ran with him." A surprised Peters nodded in agreement.

"The pace in the beginning was very fast. I was so tired and Jim was running like he could do this forever," recalled Zátopek.

"I couldn't believe what was happening," said Zátopek, "so I said to him, 'Isn't the pace too fast?' Jim said in jest, 'No, it's too slow'. . . so I believed him. So rather than wait for Jim, I ran faster and left him behind. I just kept on running and when I entered the stadium the 80,000 people were screaming 'Zátopek. . . Zátopek . . . Zátopek,' and I won my third gold medal in Helsinki. After I crossed the finish line, they told me that Jim Peters collapsed from exhaustion along the route and they had to take him to the hospital."

But of all the greatness attached to Zátopek, nothing could compare to his meeting Ron Clarke of Australia, who was the favorite to win several gold medals in the 1964 and 1968 Olympics, but in the six distance events could garner only a single bronze medal.

Zátopek truly believed that Clarke was one of the greats of all time who had a record of winning and setting world records, eighteen to be exact, whenever he ran. . . *except* at the Olympics.

One day while Clarke was visiting Zátopek, the great Czech champion handed Clarke a small box that the Australian believed was a gift. Zátopek told him not to open it untill he was on the plane going home.

When Clarke finally opened the package he saw it was one of Zátopek's Olympic gold medals. Attached to it was a card which read:

"Dear Ron, I have won four gold medals. It is only right that you should have one of them. Your friend, Emil."

Medal of Eternal Friendship

The scene was an eerie one on August 5, 1936, at the Berlin Olympic Stadium. It was a little past nine in the evening and a few lights illuminated the pole vault area where the competition had continued longer than expected. Unlike today, the Berlin Olympic Stadium had no high-intensity lighting that could turn night into day. A few thousand spectators sat in darkness to witness the climax of a very close competition.

The final four competitors sat on chairs. They were weary and cold and each covered himself with a blanket to ward off the chill. A light mist gave the scene a Wagnerian image. After Bill Sefton of the U.S.A. was eliminated, the three finalists battling for the medals were Earl Meadows of the United States and two close friends from Japan, Shuhei Nishida and Sueo Oe.

For Nishida this would be his second successive chance to win the gold medal. Four years earlier at the 1932 Los Angeles Games he had to settle for the silver medal, losing by a half an inch.

The bar stood at the Olympic record of 14 feet 3 1/4 inches. In rotation the three took their turns at clearing the height. On his second try Earl Meadows cleared. Nishida and Oe missed all three attempts. As the crowd cheered Meadows, Nishida and Oe ran over to the winner to congratulate

him. The two Japanese then continued to jump for second and third place, but darkness ended the competition before a final outcome could be determined.

"Oe and I went back to the Olympic Village certain we had tied, since we both jumped identical heights," Nishida remembered. Today ties are broken by the vaulter who has the fewest "misses" during the competition, but that rule was not in effect in 1936.

Overnight officials decided to award the silver medal to Nishida for reasons never fully explained. Oe was awarded the bronze.

"I awoke the next morning to find out that I was awarded the silver medal and my teammate Oe the bronze," said Nishida, his thoughts returning to six decades ago. "Thus I had won my second silver medal, for that was my placing four years earlier in Los Angeles. But I was not happy with the decision. When we got back to Japan both Oe and I agreed that we would have our silver and bronze medals cut in half. Then we joined half of the silver medal with half of the bronze medal which we would both keep. This made us very famous, for the medals were called the Medals of Eternal Friendship.

Sadly these are the remaining memories I have of my friend and teammate Sueo Oe, because he was killed in the Philippine campaign at the start of World War II. But his memory lives on for all of Japan. His medal remains on display at the National Stadium in Tokyo."

Modern Olympic Sites

	Year	Site	Nations	Total	Men	Women
1st Olympiad	1896	Athens, Greece	14	ca 245	ca 245	0
2nd Olympiad	1900	Paris, France	26	1,225	1,206	19
3rd Olympiad	1904	St. Louis, Missouri	13	687	681	6
Intercalated Games	1906*	Athens, Greece	20	884	877	7
4th Olympiad	1908	London, England	22	2,035	1,999	36
5th Olympiad	1912	Stockholm, Sweden	28	2,547	2,490	57
6th Olympiad	1916	*Canceled due to WWI*				
7th Olympiad	1920	Antwerp, Belgium	29	2,668	2,591	77
8th Olympiad	1924	Paris, France	44	3,092	2,956	136
9th Olympiad	1928	Amsterdam, Netherlands	46	3,014	2,724	290
10th Olympiad	1932	Los Angeles, California	37	1,408	1,281	127
11th Olympiad	1936	Berlin, Germany	49	4,066	3,738	328
12th Olympiad	1940	*Canceled due to WWII*				
13th Olympiad	1944	*Canceled due to WWII*				
14th Olympiad	1948	London, England	59	4,099	3,714	385
15th Olympiad	1952	Helsinki, Finland	69	4,925	4,407	518
16th Olympiad	1956	Melbourne, Australia	72	3,342	2,958	384
17th Olympiad	1960	Rome, Italy	83	5,346	4,738	610
18th Olympiad	1964	Tokyo, Japan	93	5,140	4,457	683
19th Olympiad	1968	Mexico City, Mexico	112	5,530	4,750	781
20th Olympiad	1972	Munich, Federal Republic of Germany	121	7,123	6,065	1,058
21st Olympiad	1976	Montreal, Canada	92	6,028	4,781	1,247
22nd Olympiad	1980	Moscow, USSR	80	5,217	4,092	1,125
23rd Olympiad	1984	Los Angeles, California	140	6,797	5,230	1,567
24th Olympiad	1988	Seoul, Republic of Korea	159	8,465	6,279	2,186
25th Olympiad	1992	Barcelona, Spain	169	9,367	6,659	2,708
26th Olympiad	1996	Atlanta, Georgia	(est) 197	10,000		
27th Olympiad	2000	Sydney, Australia				

Olympic Winter Games

	Year	Site	Nations	Total	Men	Women
Winter Events**	1908	London, England	5	21	14	7
Winter Events**	1920	Antwerp, Belgium	10	86	74	12
1st Winter Games	1924	Chamonix, France	16	258	245	13
2nd Winter Games	1928	St. Moritz, Switzerland	25	464	438	26
3rd Winter Games	1932	Lake Placid, New York	17	252	231	21
4th Winter Games	1936	Garmisch-Partenkirchen, Germany	28	668	588	80
5th Winter Games	1948	St. Moritz, Switzerland	28	669	592	77
6th Winter Games	1952	Oslo, Norway	30	694	585	109
7th Winter Games	1956	Cortina d'Ampezzo, Italy	32	820	688	132
8th Winter Games	1960	Squaw Valley, California	30	665	522	143
9th Winter Games	1964	Innsbruck, Austria	36	1,091	891	200
10th Winter Games	1968	Grenoble, France	37	1,158	947	211
11th Winter Games	1972	Sapporo, Japan	35	1,006	800	206
12th Winter Games	1976	Innsbruck, Austria	37	1,123	892	231
13th Winter Games	1980	Lake Placid, New York	37	1,072	839	233
14th Winter Games	1984	Sarajevo, Yugoslavia	49	1,274	1,000	274
15th Winter Games	1988	Calgary, Canada	57	1,423	1,110	313
16th Winter Games	1992	Albertville, France	64	1,801	1,313	488
17th Winter Games	1994	Lillehammer, Norway	67	1,844	1,302	542
18th Winter Games	1998	Nagano, Japan				
19th Winter Games	2002	Salt Lake City				

*While historians do not usually consider them to be a true Olympic Games, most acknowledge that the Intercalated Games injected new spirit into the Olympics, such as the addition of a first true Opening Ceremonies. Athletes, such as Ray Ewry later in this list, are often credited with medals won there. His lifetime total is ten medals, including the two he won in 1906; not including them, his lifetime total is eight.

**Although figure skating was an event at both the 1908 and 1920 Games, and an ice hockey tournament was contested in 1920, an authorized, official Olympic Winter Games did not emerge until 1924.

Olympic Facts

Excerpted from: *The Golden Book of the Olympic Games* by Bill Mallon and Erich Kamper • Milan, Italy • Villardi & Associati, 1993

Olympic Records

Most Medals
- 18 Larisa Latynina (URS-GYM)
- 15 Nikolay Andrianov (URS-GYM)
- 13 Edoardo Mangiarotti (ITA-FEN)
- 13 Takashi Ono (JPN-GYM)
- 13 Boris Shakhlin (URS-GYM)
- 12 Sawao Kato (JPN-GYM)
- 12 Paavo Nurmi (FIN-ATH)
- 11 Matthew Biondi (USA-SWI)
- 11 Vera Cáslavská (TCH-GYM)
- 11 Viktor Chukarin (URS-GYM)
- 11 Carl Osburn (USA-SHO)
- 11 Mark Spitz (USA-SWI)

Most Gold Medals
- 10/8 Ray Ewry (USA-ATH)*
- 9 Larisa Latynina (URS-GYM)
- 9 Paavo Nurmi (FIN-ATH)
- 9 Mark Spitz (USA-SWI)
- 8 Matthew Biondi (USA-SWI)
- 8 Sawao Kato (JPN-GYM)
- 8 Carl Lewis (USA-ATH)
- 7 Nikolay Andrianov (URS-GYM)
- 7 Vera Cáslavská (TCH-GYM)
- 7 Viktor Chukarin (URS-GYM)
- 7 Aladár Gerevich (HUN-FEN)
- 7 Boris Shakhlin (URS-GYM)

Most Silver Medals
- 6 Shirley Babashoff (USA-SWI)
- 6 Aleksandr Dityatin (URS-GYM)
- 6 Mikhail Voronin (URS-GYM)
- 5 Eleven athletes tied with five each

Most Bronze Medals
- 6 Heikki Savolainen (FIN-GYM)
- 5 Philip Edwards (CAN-ATH)
- 5 Adrianus de Jong (NED-FEN)
- 5 Daniel Revenu (FRA-FEN)
- 5 Harri Kirvesniemi (PIN-NSK)

Most Years Between Appearances
- 40 Ivan Osiier (DEN-FEN, 1908-48)
- 40 Magnus Konow (NOR-YAC, 1908-48)
- 40 Paul Elvstrom (DEN-YAC, 1948-88)
- 40 Durward Knowles (GBR/BAH-YAC, 1948-88)
- 36 Francois La Fortune Sr. (BEL-SHO, 1924-60)
- 36 Kroum Lekarski (BUL-EQU, 1924-60)
- 36 Nelson Pessoa Filho (BRA-EQU, 1956-92)

Most Medals, Women
- 18 Larisa Latynina (URS-GYM)
- 11 Vera Cáslavská (TCH-GYM)
- 10 Polina Astakhova (URS-GYM)
- 10 Àgnes Keleti (HUN-GYM)
- 10 Raisa Smetanina (URS/EUN-NSK)
- 9 Nadia Comaneci (ROM-GYM)
- 9 Lyudmila Turishcheva (URS-GYM)
- 9 Lyubov Yegorova (EUN/RUS-NSK)
- 8 Seven athletes tied with eight each

Most Gold Medals, Women
- 9 Larisa Latynina (URS-GYM)
- 7 Vera Cáslavská (TCH-GYM)
- 6 Kristin Otto (GDR-SWI)
- 6 Lidiya Skoblikova (URS-SSK)
- 6 Lyubov Yegorova (EUN/RUS-NSK)
- 5 Polina Astakhova (URS-GYM)
- 5 Polina Astakhova (URS-GYM)
- 5 Bonnie Blair (USA-SSK)
- 5 Nadia Comaneci (ROM-GYM)
- 5 Nelli Kim (URS-GYM)

Most Silver Medals, Women
- 6 Shirley Babashoff (USA-SWI)
- 5 Larisa Latynina (URS-GYM)
- 5 Mariya Gorokhovskaya (URS-GYM)
- 5 Raisa Smetanina (URS/EUN-NSK)
- 5 Andrea Ehrig-Schone-Mitscherlich (GDR-SSK)
- 4 Six athletes tied with four each

Most Bronze Medals, Women
- 4 Marja-Liisa Kirvesniemi-Hamalainen (FIN-NSK)
- 4 Margit Korondi (HUN-GYM)
- 4 Larisa Latynina (URS-GYM)
- 4 Sofiya Muratova (URS-GYM)
- 4 Merlene Otty [-Page] (JAM-ATH)
- 4 Yelena Valbe (EUN-NSK)

Most Years Winning Medals, Women
- 5 Ildikó Ságiné-Ujlakiné-Rejto (HUN-FEN)
- 5 Raisa Smetanina (URS/EUN-NSK)
- 4 Yelena Belova-Novikova (URS-FEN)
- 4 Galina Gorokhova (URS-FEN)
- 4 Galina Kulakova (URS-NSK)

4 Inna Ryskal (URS-VOL)
4 Tatyana Samusenko-Petrenko
(URS-FEN)
4 Irena Szweinska-Kirszenstein
(POL-ATH)

Most Years Winning Gold Medals, Women
3 Sixteen athletes tied with three each

Most Years Between Medals, Women
16 Ilona Elek (HUN-FEN)
16 Liselott Linsenhoff (FRG-EQU)
16 Ellen Muller-Preis (AUT-FEN)
16 Ildikó Ságiné-Ujlakiné-Rejto
(HUN-FEN)
16 Raisa Smetanina (URS/EUN-NSK)
16 Olga Szabo-Orban (ROM-FEN)

Most Years Between Gold Medals, Women
16 Raisa Smetanina (URS/EUN-NSK)
12 Seven athletes tied with twelve each

Most Appearances, Women
7 Kerstin Palm (SWE-FEN, 1964-88)
6 Janice Lee York-Romary (USA-FEN,
1964-92)
6 Lia Manoliu (ROM-ATH, 1952-72)
6 Christilot Hansen-Boylen
(CAN-EQU, 1964-76, 1984,
1992)
6 Marja-Liisa Kirvexniemi-Hamalainen
(FIN-NSK, 1976-94)
5 Twelve athletes tied with five each

Most Years Between Appearances, Women
28 Jessica Newberry-Ranschousen
(USA-EQU, 1960-88)
28 Christilot Hansen-Boylen
(CAN-EQU, 1964-92)
24 Ellen Muller-Preis (AUT-FEN,
1932-56)
20 Seven athletes tied with 20 each

Most Medals, Men
15 Nikolay Andrianov (URS-GYM)
13 Edoardo Mangiarotti (ITA-FEN)
13 Takashi Ono (JPN-GYM)
13 Boris Shakhlin (URS-GYM)
12 Sawao Kato (JPN-GYM)
12 Paavo Nurmi (FIN-ATH)

Most Gold Medals, Men
10/8 Ray Ewry (USA-ATH)*
9 Paavo Nurmi (FIN-ATH)
9 Mark Spitz (USA-SWI)
8 Matthew Biondi (USA-SWI)
8 Sawao Kato (JPN-GYM)
8 Carl Lewis (USA-ATH)

Most Silver Medals, Men
6 Mikhail Voonin (URS-GYM)
6 Aleksander Dityatin (URS-GYM)
5 Seven athletes tied with five each

Most Bronze Medals, Men
6 Heikki Savolainen (FIN-GYM)
5 Philip Edwards (CAN-ATH)
5 Adrianus de Jong (NED-FEN)
5 Daniel Revenu (FRA-FEN)
4 Nine athletes tied with four each

Most Years Winning Medals, Men
6 Aladár Gerevich (HUN-FEN)
6 Hans Gunter Winkler (FRG-EQU)
5 Ten athletes tied with five each

Most Years Between Medals, Men
28 Aladár Gerevich (HUN-FEN)
28 Alfréd Hajós (HUN-SWI/ART)
28 Tore Holm (SWE-YAC)
24 Eight athletes tied with 24 each

Most Years Between Gold Medals, Men
28 Aladár Gerevich (HUN-FEN)
24 Reiner Klimke (FRG/GER-EQU)
24 Pál Kovács (HUN-FEN)
24 Edoardo Mangiarotti (ITA-FEN)
20 Manlio Di Rosa (ITA-FEN)
20 Lars Jorgen Madsen (DEN-SHO)

20 Hubert Van Innis (BEL-ARC)

Most Appearances, Men
8 Paul Elvstrom (DEN-YAC, 1948-60, 1968-72, 1984-88)
8 Raimondo d'Inzco (ITA-EQU, 1948-76)
8 Durward Knowles (GBR/BAH-YAC, 1948-72, 1988)
8 Hubert Raudaschi (AUT-YAC, 1964-92)
8 Piero d'Inzco (ITA-EQU, 1948-76)
7 Four athletes tied with seven each

Most Years Between Appearances, Men
40 Ivan Osiier (DEN-FEN, 1908-1948)
40 Magnus Konow (NOR-YAC, 1908-48)
40 Paul Elvstórm (DEN-YAC, 1948-88)
40 Durward Knowles (GBR/BAH-YAC, 1948-88)
36 Francois La Fortune, Sr. (BEL-SHO, 1924-60)
36 Kroum Lekarski (BUL-EQU, 1924-1960)
36 Nelson Pessoa Filho (BRA-EQU, 1956-92)

Youngest Medalist, Overall
(age in years and days)
<10 Unknown French boy* in 1900 (ROW)
10-218 Dimitrios Loundreas (GRE-GYM, 1896)
11-302 Luigina Giavotti (ITA-GYM, 1928)
12-024 Inge Sorensen (DEN-SWI, 1936)
12-218 Ines Vercesi (ITA- GYM, 1928)
12-233 Noel Vandernotte (FRA-ROW, 1936)
12-271 Clara Marangoni (ITA-GYM, 1928)
13-024 Dorothy Poynton (USA-DIV, 1928)
13-283 Kim Yoon-Mi (KOR-STK, 1994)
13-268 Marjorie Gestring (USA-DIV, 1936)

Youngest Known Competitors, Overall
<10 Unknown French boy* in 1900 (ROW)
10-218 Dimitrios Loundreas (GRE-GYM, 1896)
11-078 Cecilia Colledge (GBR-FSK, 1932)

11-108 Megan Taylor (GBR-FSK, 1932)
11-162 Beatrice Hustiu (ROM-FSK, 1968)

*The Dutch coxed pairs (rowing) qualified with a heavy coxswain, and then picked a small boy from the shore to sit in the cox's seat for the final. The team won.

Oldest Medalist, Overall
72-279 Oscar Swahn (SWE-SHO, 1920)
68-193 Samuel Duvall (USA-ARC, 1904)
66-155 Louis Noverraz (SUI-YAC, 1968)
64-257 Oscar Swahn (SWE-SHO, 1912)
64-001 Galen Spencer (USA-ARC, 1904)
63-239 Robert Williams (USA-ARC, 1904)
61-244 John Butt (GBR-SHO, 1912)
61-131 Bill Roycroft (AUS-EQU, 1976)
60-264 Oscar Swahn (SWE-SHO, 1908)
60-103 William Milne (GBR-SHO, 1912)

Oldest Known Competitors, Overall
72-280 Oscar Swahn (SWE-SHO, 1920)
72-048 Arthur von Pongracz (AUT-EQU, 1936)
70-330 Durward Knowles (BAH-YAC, 1988)
70-005 Lorna Johnstone (GBR-EQU, 1972)
68-229 Roberto Soundy (ESA-SHO, 1968)

Official Country Abbreviations

AFG Afghanistan	DEN Denmark	LAO Laos	SEY Seychelles
AHO Neth. Antilles	DJI Djibouti	LAT Latvia	SIN Singapore
ALB Albania	DOM Dominican Republic	LBA Libya	SLE Sierra Leone
ALG Algeria	ECU Ecuador	LBR Liberia	SLO Slovenia
AND Andorra	EGY Egypt	LES Lesotho	SMR San Marino
ANG Angola	ESA El Salvador	LIB Lebanon	SMY Smyrna
ANL Antilles (W. Indies)	ESP Spain	LIE Liechtenstein	SOL Solomon Islands
ANT Antigua	EST Estonia	LTU Lithuania	SOM Somalia
ARG Argentina	EUN Unified Team (CIS)	LUX Luxembourg	SRI Sri Lanka
ARM Armenia	FIJ Fiji	MAD Madagascar	SUD The Sudan
ARU Aruba	FIN Finland	MAR Morocco	SUI Switzerland
ASA American Samoa	FRA France	MAL Malaysia	SUR Suriname
AUS Australia	FRG Federal Rep. of	MAW Malawi	SVK Slovakia
AUT Austria	Germany	MCD Macedonia	SWE Sweden
AZE Azerbaijan	GAB Gabon	MDV Maldives	SWZ Swaziland
BAH The Bahamas	GAM The Gambia	MEX Mexico	SYR Syria
BAN Bangladesh	GBR Great Britain	MGL Mongolia	TAN Tanzania
BAR Barbados	GDR German Demo. Rep.	MLD Moldova	TCH Czechoslovakia
BEL Belgium	GEO Georgia	MLI Mali	TGA Tonga
BEN Benin	GEQ Equatorial Guinea	MLT Malta	THA Thailand
BER Bermuda	GER Germany	MON Monaco	TJK Tadzhikistan
BHU Bhutan	GHA Ghana	MOZ Mozambique	TKM Turkmenistan
BIR Burma	GRE Greece	MRI Mauritius	TOG Togo
BIZ Belize	GRN Grenada	MTN Mauritania	TPE Chinese Taipei
BLS Belarus	GUA Guatemala	MYA Myanmar	TRI Trinidad & Tobago
BOH Bohemia	GUI Guinea	NAM Namibia	TSL Thessalonika
BOL Bolivia	GUM Guam	NCA Nicaragua	TUN Tunisia
BOT Botswana	GUY Guyana	NED The Netherlands	TUR Turkey
BRA Brazil	HAI Haiti	NEP Nepal	UAE United Arab Emirates
BRN Bahrain	HKG Hong Kong	NGR Nigeria	UES USSR/Estonia
BRU Brunei	HON Honduras	NIG Niger	UGA Uganda
BSH Bosnia-Herzegovina	HUN Hungary	NOR Norway	UKR The Ukraine
BUL Bulgaria	INA Indonesia	NZL New Zealand	ULA USSR/Latvia
BUR Burkina-Faso	IND India	OMA Oman	ULI USSR/Lithuania
CAM Kampuchea	IOP Independent Olympic	PAK Pakistan	URS Soviet Union
CAN Canada	Participant	PAN Panama	URU Uruguay
CAY Cayman Islands	IRI Iran	PAR Paraguay	USA United States
CEY Ceylon	IRL Ireland	PER Peru	UZB Uzbekistan
CGO Congo	IRQ Iraq	PHI The Philippines	VAN Vanuatu
CHA Chad	ISL Iceland	PNG Papua New Guinea	VEN Venezuela
CHI Chile	ISR Israel	POL Poland	VIE Vietnam
CHN China	ISV U.S. Virgin Islands	POR Portugal	VIN St. Vincent &
CIS Commonwealth of	ITA Italy	PRK DPR Korea (North)	the Grenadines
Independent States	IVB British Virgin Islands	PUR Puerto Rico	VOL Upper Volta
CIV Ivory Coast	JAM Jamaica	QAT Qatar	YAR Yemen AR (North)
CMR Cameroon	JOR Jordan	RHO Rhodesia	YEM Yemen
COK Cook Islands	JPN Japan	ROM Romania	YMD Yemen DR (South)
COL Colombia	KEN Kenya	RUS Russia	YUG Yugoslavia
CRC Costa Rica	KGZ Kergizstan	RWA Rwanda	ZAI Zaire
CRO Croatia	KOR Korea (South)	SAF South Africa	ZAM Zambia
CUB Cuba	KSA Saudi Arabia	SAM Western Samoa	ZIM Zimbabwe
CYP Cyprus	KUW Kuwait	SCO Scotland	
CZE Czech Republic	KZK Kazakhstan	SEN Senegal	

Three-Letter Sport Abbreviations

ARC Archery	FTB Football Association (Soccer)	RUG Rugby Football
ASK Alpine Skiing	GYM Gymnastics	SHO Shooting
ATH Athletic (Track & Field)	HAN Team Handball	SKE Skeleton
BAS Basketball	HOK Hockey (Field)	SSK Speed Skating
BIA Biathlon	ICH Ice Hockey	SWI Swimming
BOB Bobsledding	JUD Judo	TEN Tennis (Lawn Tennis)
BOX Boxing	LAX Lacrosse	TOW Tug-of-War
CAN Canoe & Kayaking	LUG Luge	TTN Table Tennis
CYC Cycling	MOP Modern Pentathlon	VOL Volleyball
DIV Diving	MTB Motorboating	WAP Water Polo
EQU Equestrian Events	NSK Nordic Skiing	WLT Weightlifting
FEN Fencing	POL Polo	WRE Wrestling
FSK Figure Skating	ROW Rowing and Sculling	YAC Yachting

Olympic Ceremonies and Traditions

Olympic Flag

The Olympic flag has a plain white background with no border. In the center are five interconnected rings. They form two rows of three rings above and two below. The rings of the upper row are, from left to right, blue, black and red. The rings of the lower row are yellow and green.

The rings are thought to symbolize the five continents, Europe, Asia, Africa, Australia and America. The colors of the rings are thought to have been chosen because at least one of these colors can be found in the flag of every nation. It is not certain that this was the intent of the flag's designer.

The flag was presented by Baron Pierre de Coubertin in 1914 at the Olympic Congress in 1914, celebrating the 20th anniversary of the founding of the International Olympic Committee. It was flown that year at Alexandria, Greece, but made its Olympic début in 1920 at Antwerp. The "primary" Olympic flag was thus known as "the Antwerp flag." In 1984, Seoul presented a new Olympic flag (as the old was getting quite worn) to the IOC, which was first flown at the 1988 Olympics.

At the closing ceremonies of the Olympic Games, the mayor of the Olympic host city presents the Olympic flag to the mayor of the next Olympic host city. The flag is then kept in the town hall of the host city until the next Olympic Games.

Olympic Motto

"Citius, altius, fortius" — a Latin phrase meaning "swifter, higher, stronger." De Coubertin adopted it after hearing of its use by Father Henri Martin Didon of Paris. Didon, later headmaster of Arcueil College, used the phrase while describing the athletic accomplishments of his students at that school. He had previously been at the Albert Le Grand school, where the Latin words were carved in stone above the main entrance.

Olympic Creed

"The most important thing in the Olympic Games is not to win but to take part, just as the most important thing in life is not the triumph, but the struggle. The essential thing is not to have conquered but to have fought well."

This is the current form of the creed as it appears on the scoreboard at the Opening Ceremonies of the Olympic Games, although many permutations of this basic message have been seen.

De Coubertin adopted, and later quoted, this creed after hearing Ethelbert Talbot, the Bishop of Central Pennsylvania, speak at St. Paul's Cathedral on July 19, 1908, during the London Olympics. The service was given for the Olympic athletes, who were all invited.

Talbot was in London for the 5th Conference of Anglican Bishops (usually called the Lambeth Conference). During the conference, many of the visiting bishops spoke in various churches. Talbot's exact words that day were:

"The important thing in these Olympics is not so much winning as taking part."

Olympic Oath

"In the name of all competitors, I promise that we shall take part in these Olympic Games, respecting and abiding by the rules which govern them, in the true spirit of sportsmanship, for the glory of sport and the honor of our teams."

Written by de Coubertin, the oath is taken by an athlete from the host country, while holding a corner of the Olympic flag. It is also given by a judge from the host country, with slightly different wording. The athlete's oath was first given in 1920 in Antwerp by Belgian fencer Victor Boin.

The original wording ended with "countries," but it was changed in the 1960s because of the IOC's desire to eliminate nationalism at the Olympics.

Olympic Flame

The Olympic flame is a symbol reminiscent of the ancient Olympics, in which a sacred flame burned at the altar of Zeus throughout the Olympics. The flame was first used at the modern Olympics in Amsterdam in 1928, and again was lit throughout the 1932 Los Angeles Olympics.

In 1936, Carl Diem, chairman of the organizing committee for the Berlin Olympics, proposed the idea of lighting the flame in ancient Greece and transporting it to Berlin via torch relay. This was done and has been repeated at every Olympic Winter Games since 1952.

The flame is lit in the altis of the ancient Olympic stadium at ancient Olympia, on the Greek Peloponnesus. The flame is lit during a ceremony by women dressed in robes similar to those worn by the ancient Greeks. The flame is lit naturally by the rays of the sun at Olympia and reflected off a curved mirror. A symbolic high priestess then presents the torch to the first relay runner.

This work could not have been completed without the help of three expert collections: ALLSPORT (U.S.A. & U.K.), the United States Olympic Committee and the Amateur Athletic Foundation of Los Angeles. Individual credits, as required, follow: